D0990360

BOOKS BY MAX EASTMAN

SEVEN KINDS OF GOODNESS
LOVE AND REVOLUTION
ENJOYMENT OF LIVING
ENJOYMENT OF POETRY
JOURNALISM VERSUS ART
UNDERSTANDING GERMANY
THE SENSE OF HUMOR
SINCE LENIN DIED
LEON TROTSKY, THE PORTRAIT OF A YOUTH
MARX AND LENIN, THE SCIENCE OF REVOLUTION
VENTURE, A NOVEL
THE LITERARY MIND, ITS PLACE IN AN AGE OF SCIENCE
ARTISTS IN UNIFORM
ART AND THE LIFE OF ACTION
ENJOYMENT OF LAUGHTER
THE END OF SOCIALISM IN RUSSIA
STALIN'S RUSSIA AND THE CRISIS IN SOCIALISM
MARXISM IS IT SCIENCE?
HEROES I HAVE KNOWN
REFLECTIONS ON THE FAILURE OF SOCIALISM
GREAT COMPANIONS, A CRITICAL MEMOIR OF SOME FAMOUS FRIENDS

Poetry

CHILD OF THE AMAZONS AND OTHER POEMS
COLORS OF LIFE
KINDS OF LOVE
LOT'S WIFE, A DRAMATIC POEM
POEMS OF FIVE DECADES

Translations

THE REAL SITUATION IN RUSSIA *by Leon Trotsky*
GABRIEL *by Pushkin*
THE HISTORY OF THE RUSSIAN REVOLUTION *by Leon Trotsky*
THE REVOLUTION BETRAYED *by Leon Trotsky*

Edited

CAPITAL AND OTHER WRITINGS *by Karl Marx*
ANTHOLOGY FOR "THE ENJOYMENT OF POETRY"
TZAR TO LENIN, A MOVING-PICTURE HISTORY OF THE RUSSIAN REVOLUTION

SEVEN KINDS OF GOODNESS

MAX EASTMAN

SEVEN KINDS OF GOODNESS

HORIZON PRESS NEW YORK

Library of Congress Catalog Card Number: 67–17781
Manufactured in the United States of America

CONTENTS

The Plight of Moral Ideals
page 11

I Buddha: The Enlightened One
page 17

II The Teacher of Growth: Confucius
page 31

III The Mosaic Dictatorship
page 45

IV Socrates: The Herald of Logic
page 67

V The Champion of Intelligence: Plato
page 79

VI The Two Lives of Mohammed
page 101

VII Jesus As a Human Teacher
page 119

The Cardinal Virtues: An Un-Sabbath-Day Sermon
page 139

Appendix: The Reality of Choice and Judgment
page 153

ACKNOWLEDGMENTS

Four of the essays in this book, the ones on Buddha, Confucius, Socrates, and Plato, were published, in a condensed form, in the *Reader's Digest.* The essay on "The Cardinal Virtues" was published in *The American Scholar.* My thanks are due to these magazines for publishing them, and for permission to republish them. The conversation with Einstein from which I quote in the appendix was published in my book *Great Companions,* copyright © 1942, 1959, reprinted with permission of the publishers, Farrar, Straus and Giroux, Inc.

M. E.

ACKNOWLEDGMENTS

[illegible]

M. B.

THE PLIGHT OF MORAL IDEALS

THE PLIGHT OF MORAL IDEALS

The idea that moral standards derive their validity from a belief in God, or in a future life, although a fanciful idea, seems to be taken for granted by most Americans. They associate morality with religion almost as a matter of course. This is especially unfortunate today because the beliefs in God and in a future life are losing their firm seat in our minds. More and more the prayer with which some priest or parson opens a political convention, or the sessions of a legislature, seems irrelevant, incongruous, even a little embarrassing. This fact is psychological, and statistics of church membership and attendance have no bearing on it. To be "a believer" is one thing—it is a matter of status in this world; to *believe* that an Unseen Power in another world actually watches over you, guiding your steps, is another. There are many "believers"; there are few who believe.

In the long run this coming down to earth of our thoughts

about the conduct of life will, I think, make us behave more wisely. If the run is long enough, there is little doubt of that. But the immediate effect on those brought up to believe that moral standards are set up by God, and that good conduct finds its reward and sanction only in a future life, is apt to be damaging. For them the ideal of personal virtue is losing some of its commanding force.

In the communist half of the world, where the belief in God and a future life is denounced by a state religion, the codes of individual morality are in a still more shaky position. Karl Marx was so sure that the world was going to be redeemed by its own dialectic evolution that he would not permit his disciples to invoke the guidance of moral ideals. He really meant it when he said that the workers have "no ideal to realize," they have only to participate in the contemporary class struggle. He expelled people from his Communist Party for mentioning programmatically such things as love, justice, humanity, even morality itself. "Soulful ravings," "sloppy sentimentality," he called such expressions, and purged the astonished authors as though they had committed the most dastardly crimes.

Lenin gave the following instruction to a youth congress in Moscow on October 4, 1920:

"We reject all morality derived from superhuman or superclass conceptions. For us morality is entirely subordinate to the class struggle of the proletariat. Our morality is deduced from the interests of the class struggle of the proletariat."

Trotsky made the same leap from a rejection of "transcendental morality" to the rejection of all moral standards except loyalty to the class struggle for the dictatorship of the proletariat. Stalin, Khrushchev and the others have acted, politically at least, on the same principle. Apparently it has not occurred to any of them that, on those grounds, once the proletarian society is achieved, no "morality," no standards of honorable and good conduct, will have any validity at all.

I must not seem to compare the plight of moral ideals among Communists with their adventitiously declining authority among us. The professedly scientific, but in reality religious, belief of the Communists that the material world is evolving with historic necessity, and without regard for human scruples, to a future paradise where everybody will be good and happy gives their disaffection from moral ideals a status that ours lacks. Their god—the dialectic universe—demands it. But under the banners of that god they have conquered almost half the world, and their influence in the other half, both emotional and through conspiratorial contact, is insidious. Even those among us who reject both the Hebrew God and the Marxian hoax of Dialectic Materialism, are apt to be vague about the validity of moral standards. Thus on both sides the idea of personal virtue, of living a good life, seems to be hanging in the air. Yet if civilization is worth preserving it is quite possibly the most important of all the ideas that have ever arisen in men's minds.

It may be profitable, in these circumstances, to glance back at a few of those historic characters who were so possessed by this idea, and so dwelt upon it that, for better or worse, they became moral law-givers for whole epochs or peoples. Buddha, Confucius, Moses, Mohammed, Socrates, Plato, Jesus—suppose we enter for a brief view into the mind of each of these seven men, judging them as teachers of a good life in this world, not as prophets of God or of something that may be imagined to happen in the next. It will remind us, at least, of the enticing variety and complexities of the need for goodness, and the infantine folly of sweeping it aside in a march to political power.

I

BUDDHA

BUDDHA: THE ENLIGHTENED ONE

Images of Buddha are as numerous in many parts of Asia as crucifixes in Christendom, and they command the same reverence. They are rather plump images. To us Buddha seems a little well-fed and complacent for a Holy man. We expect the saints to do some agonizing in their search for the inner light. But so did Buddha's friends and those to whom he preached. Indeed the idea of illumination through suffering reached its peak of popularity in India in the age, six hundred years before Christ, in which he lived. It was almost a fad for young men, harassed and puzzled by the sorrows in the world, to wind up their affairs, say a bland or passionate farewell to their families, and "go forth"—or as we should say, *walk out.* They would live in the woods like owls or jackals, their only possessions the wooden bowls with which they would come out on the road from time to time and beg a bite to eat. It would be only a morsel, for their idea was that self-mortification, if persisted in, would bring on a moment of ecstatic perception in which the whole secret of the universe would become suddenly clear.

The first revolutionary thing about Buddha was that he tried this and decided it was foolish. He had been a prince in a small Indian kingdom, and was twenty-nine years old, married and the father of a baby son, before he walked out.* And he went at midnight without a word to anybody, fearing he would take too much of them with him if he said goodbye to his wife and child. It was anguish to him—he stood a moment beside the bed on which they lay sleeping, but turned away. His will was iron, and from being a prince of this world, he became the prince of ascetics, so zealous in self-mortification that his fame spread abroad "like the sound of a great gong hung up in the sky."

He had five companions in this enterprise, but they were so impressed by his superior gift of application that they mostly just sat around and watched him do it. One day when he had reduced himself to a faltering skeleton, and practiced suppressed breathing until he was black in the face, instead of receiving the expected illumination he was attacked by violent pains and fell in a dead faint. When he came to, he decided that in order to crack the secrets of the universe you have to keep yourself in fairly good health.

* Gotama was his personal name. Buddha, "the Enlightened One," is a title like Messiah, except that there are supposed to have been other Buddhas in the remote past, and still others are supposed to appear in the future.

You have to adopt a "middle way" between ascetic self-denial and sensual indulgence. To us the surprise is that it took him six years in the woods to get hold of this bit of obvious good sense. But in the religious culture of India in those days it was a revolution. Gotama was denounced as a quitter by his five cronies and had to continue his search for the ultimate wisdom all alone.

It must be remarked that Gotama's middle way was, from the viewpoint of American morals and dietetics, well to the left of the middle. His chastity was absolute and his big meal, taken at noon, consisted of curry and rice and after that nothing solid—perhaps a little gruel for supper. He throve on this, however, and became not only a well-filled-out saint such as you see in the statues, but an intellectual athlete besides. Indeed Gotama has a place in the history of philosophy as well as of religion. He wrestled with those same ultimate problems of mind and matter, being and becoming, which we think of as first tackled by the ancient Greeks, and he wrestled as sturdily as they. It is said of Socrates that he stood thinking in a portico all of one night. The same thing is reported of Gotama except that he had the forethought to sit down. He sat under a pipal tree, afterwards called Tree of Knowledge—Bo Tree in Singhalese. That tree has been replanted from its own seeds throughout the ages, and you can still see it in the Indian village of Buddh Gaya if you go there with a believing heart.

Gotama made up his mind when he sat down under the

Bo Tree that he would never get up until he received an illumination. That would prevent most of us from receiving one, but it worked the other way with Gotama. Toward the small hours he fell into a trance in which he beheld with a kind of incandescent clarity the whole intricate concatenation of causes and effects which regulates this misery called life. And he beheld with the same clarity the path of deliverance into bliss.

These mystic experiences are, as a rule, irresistibly convincing to those who undergo them. Gotama, when he got up after his night under the Bo Tree, had no hesitation in proclaiming himself not only Buddha, the "Enlightened," but also Tathagata, the "Perfect One." He went straight back to those five hermits who had denounced him, and who were still starving themselves in a deer park at Benares. They were far from receptive when they saw him coming.

"Let's show no respect to this renegade," they said, "this convert to self-indulgence. We'll leave a seat for him, but we won't stand up or take his cloak and bowl."

As the illuminated Gotama came nearer, however, they lost their nerve and rushed out in a body to meet him. One took his cloak and bowl; another prepared a seat; a third gave him a footstool and water to wash his feet. And they addressed him by name and called him "Brother."

He answered—it is hard to believe without a glint of triumph in his eye—"O monks, address not Tathagata by his name and call him not 'Brother.' Tathagata, O monks, is the holy and supreme Buddha. Open your ears, O monks! . . . If you walk according to my teaching, you shall in this present life possess that for which noble youths leave home and go into homelessness, that supreme truth which is the aim of all religious effort."

Then Gotama, the Buddha, preached a sermon—propably with one exception the most momentous sermon ever preached. Like the Sermon on the Mount, the Sermon in the Deer Park presented in succinct outline a new way of life. The two ways of life, Christian and Buddhist, are surprisingly similar, though the beliefs they rest on are wide apart. In Buddha's gospel there is no God; prayer has no efficacy; man has no soul; immortality is a vain notion; there exists no permanent or eternal thing. The old Hindu religion had arrived at the idea of One God, a First Cause beyond or behind the seemingly endless chain of causes and effects; Buddha, though reared in that religion, was not interested in this static cause. For him there was only the endless chain. The soul or ego he dismissed as a childish delusion, explaining how it arises much as a modern Behaviorist might. He denounced the craving for immortality in the same breath with the lusts of the flesh. And he accepted with a serene pessimism not unlike that of Ecclesiastes the universality of change and decay. Indeed, Buddha's pessimism outdoes that of Ecclesiastes, for his condemnation of life is not negative—not "all is vanity"—but *all is misery*.

I don't know why it is that the people of India find it natural to regard life as an affliction—whether they lack playful humor, lack vital energy, or actually are, so much more than we, beset by poverty, disease, and early death. Perhaps if we believed as they do in the monotonously recurring cycle of reincarnation, we should not find life so brisk an adventure. We conceive ourselves as going somewhere even though to oblivion. But they are just eternally turning up again and again with another face and body.

At any rate, Buddha's discovery under the Bo Tree was that the cause of our misery is ignorance. We don't know what we're talking about. We talk about selves, and we are always craving satisfactions for something we call self. But there is no self. Selves are merely transitory formations crystallized out of the general flux of things and events. We must cut off and abandon this delusion of selfhood and the ignorant cravings that go with it—specifically, "craving for the gratification of the passions, craving for a future life, craving for success in this life." We must learn, through liberation of our minds from superstition, through the austere disciplining of our wills, and through love, to interflow with the world and be humble and unhankering parts of it. In this lies peace and perfect happiness.

Buddha would have made a good bookkeeper, for he loved to arrange things in neat little lists with numbers attached to them: the four noble truths, the eight-fold path of salvation, the ten fetters that hold us back from The Path, the seven stages of consciousness, the nine grades of being, the fifteen holy practices, the four trances of contemplation, etc. It seems a little old-maidish to us; his ten fetters and eight-fold path have none of the free-spoken eloquence of the Beatitudes. They might well be reproduced in that form, however, for *Beatitude and How to Reach It* was the central theme of his teachings.

Blessed are they who *know*, he would begin, and whose knowledge is free from delusion and superstition.

Blessed are they who speak what they know in a kindly, open and truthful manner.

Blessed are they who aspire—or, as we should say, hunger and thirst—after goodness.

Blessed are they whose conduct is peaceful, honest and pure.

Blessed are they who earn their living in a way that brings hurt or danger to no living thing.

Blessed are the adequately fed, clothed, bathed and comfortable, provided they are not intoxicated and not tainted by sensual lust.

Blessed are the tranquil, who have cast out ill-will, pride, self-righteousness, and put in their place love, pity and sympathy.

Blessed are ye when ye direct your main efforts to self-training and self-control.

Blessed beyond measure, when by this means ye are unwrapped from the limitations of selfhood altogether.

And blessed, finally, when ye find rapture in contemplating what is deeply and really true about this world and our life in it. (Blessed, so to speak, are the philosophers.)

It is, you see, a rather austere and solemn gospel. I find no "consider the lilies" in the Buddhist scriptures, and only one glimmer of what might be called a humorous smile.* That is where Gotama decides at last, under high pressure from his converted and fanatically consecrated foster-mother, to admit women into the Buddhist Order. He turns to his beloved disciple and says (in effect):

Ananda, but for that decision I just made, this religion we are founding might have lasted a thousand years. Now I give it five hundred at the outside!

Buddha did seriously affirm that his teaching was transitory, that his religion would perish from the earth. He even described the exact order in which the different parts of it would drop out of men's minds. Perhaps he sensed dimly a fault that others have found in his system: the excessive coolness of its ideal; "to live unattached, nor cling to anything in this world." For he predicted the coming of another Buddha who would again point the way of salvation, and confided that the name of this future savior would be the "Friendly One."

Notwithstanding this modest opinion of its founder, Buddhism became in a few centuries the religion of a good third of the human race. It is still adhered to by five or six hundred millions of men and women. Like all high teachings it has, of course, been vulgarized through the ages to accommodate infantile minds. A large proportion of those

* An amateurish opinion. Those scriptures are twice as long as the Bible, and I am far from pretending to have read them all.

who bring flowers to the shrines of Buddha worship this atheist under the impression that he is himself a god. There are, however, many thoughtful and scholarly people in Asia who believe in the old pure philosophical religion of Buddhism.

Buddha's intense moralism is one of the reasons for this. Although he did not believe in God, he believed in a moral order such as only a just and omnipotent deity could ordain. He believed that every good act brings a reward, every evil act a retribution, either to you in your present person, or to a new being who will inherit your moral character when you die. By piling up "merit" with good deeds you can elevate the status of this future being who is both you and not you, and by piling them up to the point of perfection, you can escape from the cycle of reincarnation altogether.

The universe is not divine, it is not personal, but it is just—it is moral to the last fiber. That was Buddha's atheism. Be as matter-of-fact, as sceptical, pessimistic, cynical even, as you will, but just the same—be good! For no matter what you do with your mind or body, you can not escape the moral law. You can not wriggle out of it either by sophistry or suicide.

Buddha rejected, along with the belief in one or many gods, the practice of priestly rites and sacrifices. He stood like an intellectual rock against mumbo-jumbo. But in that rapt philosophic contemplation of reality which stands at the summit of his eightfold-path he provided a kind of substitute for divine communion. It is not prayer, but it is the thing most often successfully prayed for: resignation. It is a surrender of selfhood leading to an almost superhuman tranquillity. Although agreed that life in its crude form is pain and pathos, Buddha's followers become lyrical in extolling the joy of walking out of it along the eightfold-path to this serene condition.

That they could attain it without believing a great many things which free minds find it hard to believe, is one secret of the success of Buddha's religion. It is the most intellectual religion in the world. It is the most tolerant religion in the world—no priest of Buddha ever persecuted a heretic. And it is the most friendly to science, the most unafraid of doubt.

"Do not believe anything," Buddha said, "on mere hearsay; do not believe traditions because they are old and handed down through many generations; do not believe simply because the written testimony of some ancient sage is shown to you; never believe anything because presumption is in its favor or the custom of many years leads you to regard it as true; do not believe anything on the mere authority of teachers or priests. Whatever according to your own experience and after thorough investigation agrees with your reason, and is conducive to your own weal and to that of all other living things, *that* accept as truth and live accordingly."

No such words were ever spoken, before or since, by any proclaimer of a gospel. They give a very modern, very western, and, at this moment especially, a very important, meaning to those plump, calm, healthy, far-above-smiling images of Gotama, the Buddha.

For forty-five years after he received his illumination, this genius of love and meditation wandered about in the valley of the Ganges, covering a region about twice the size of Palestine, rising at dawn every morning, walking fifteen to twenty miles a day, keeping himself in perfect trim, teaching all men without recompense, without distinction of sex, color, class or caste, the way to happiness which he had found. He was no agitator, and was never molested either by the priesthood he opposed or by any ruler. He became so famous and so loved that throngs of people would come out as he approached a town and spread flowers in his path. It need not matter much what his theories about the universe were—its secrets will never be cracked by sitting under a Bo Tree. His real and triumphant aim was to define accurately and teach all men the noblest and happiest way of living and dying in this present world. To that aim he made as great a contribution as any man has made.

He was eighty years old and still traveling on foot from place to place, dressed in the yellow robes of the order he had founded, expounding his gospel and helping people to live by it, when the last sickness attacked him. His disciples spread a blanket for him between two trees in a little grove, and he lay down on his right side to die. His parting advice to them was please not to put any pope or captain in his place. Let his teachings be their only leader—an advice which has been followed through the ages. And his last words were at once the most resigned and the most resolute —certainly the most highbrow—ever spoken:

"All compound entities that come into being must cease to be. Work out your own salvation with diligence."

II

CONFUCIUS

THE TEACHER OF GROWTH: CONFUCIUS

To me there is something so alien in the looks and get-up of Confucius as portrayed by Chinese artists that I can hardly bring into my mind the towering greatness of the man. Those thick eyebrows lifting a look of surprise so irrelevantly high above the sober slits of eyes; that careful beard and moustache—and even the sideburns—hanging so far down, each in a particular strand like a stream divided by pebbles; and the costume, so near to what we call a "Japanese kimono," suggest a comic manikin rather than a mighty hero. Confucius was, however, a powerful and active man, a fervent hunter, a crack shot (that is, with a bow and arrow), a gifted musician, as well as a man of laughter and great learning. He knew as much about what there was to know as any scholar in China. And he stands alone in history as having, with only one life to live, moulded the mind and manners of a whole nation.

There was nothing in the events of his life to explain

this; it was just a matter of far-sighted wisdom combined with great personal magnetism. Although not high born, he gave sure promise even in his childhood that he would rise to high office under some duke, or perhaps under the Emperor himself. He gradually became convinced of this too. He thought he knew why things in China were so bad, and how a wise philosophy and a good government could mend them.

Things were, indeed, unbelievably bad. China in the years 551 to 470 B.C.—the life-span of Confucius—has been described by a learned historian, despairing of any more dignified expression, as "an awful mess." There was no fixed system of authority, no reign of law. A remote emperor presided over a loose collection of warring feudal dukes or princes, who settled all issues by brute force. A loser in the game of power politics might be castrated, boiled or buried alive, and his family with him. There was no thought of security even for the nobles. The people were taxed, robbed, scourged and murdered. Assassinations were frequent. Bribery was commonplace. Punishments were ferocious. Special footgear was on sale in the shops for peasants who had had their feet mutilated.

Confucius believed that these dreadful conditions could be cured, and in due time an earthly paradise produced, by teaching people the art of living. He was one of the world's supreme teachers of that art—more modestly a teacher than any of the rest of them. He was not a saint or a prophet, a stoic, an epicurean, a theist, a pantheist, any kind of an "-ist." He had no master-key to the secrets of the universe. Although his teachings are often spoken of as the religion of China, he had little interest in religion. When he seemed to be dying, one of his disciples proposed to offer a prayer.

"Is that customary?" he asked, and when assured that it was, he only smiled and said: "I did my kind of praying long ago."

By his kind of praying, I suppose he meant living a good life. But he did not think such a life would gain him admission into Heaven. Heaven was a word he used rather vaguely to indicate a sort of reflection upstairs of what we have down here on earth. If there are mysterious powers up there in the azure, they are beyond man's control, and therefore irrelevant to the problems we humans have to solve. This aggressive negligence of the supernatural gives, I think, a special value and tone-quality to everything he said about the good life. It gives, at least, a very matter-of-fact endorsement to one of the most sacred jewels of our own gospel, the Golden Rule. For Confucius was the inventor of that magical formula. When asked if he could sum up his teachings in some single word, he said:

"Wouldn't that word be reciprocity? Do not unto others what you would not have them do to you."

It sounds less generous in this negative form than our "Do unto others . . ." but it is really only a little more circumspect in phrasing. It doesn't ask us to busy ourselves imagining what other people might want. And that circumspectness is characteristic of Confucius. He was no maker of plausible epigrams.

His teachings have come down to us in the form of a vast collection of disconnected remarks and conversational episodes recorded by his pupils and disciples. Unfortunately, they are not blended with a story of his life, as are those of Jesus, and that makes them harder to read. But they also lack the reckless eloquence of the Christian gospels. Confucius disliked eloquence—except in poetry—and was suspicious of it. "As to language," he said, "it is simply required that it convey the meaning."

Sometimes he seems almost to have been correcting in advance the extravagance of the Christian gospels, and of other rather extreme statements. When asked what he thought of the principle that one should reward injury with kindness, he said: "With what, then will you reward kindness? Reward injury with justice, kindness with kindness." Although he had no reverence for the hereditary aristocracy which ruled the land in which he lived, he did not come out with the cry, "All men are created equal!" He said more carefully: "By nature men are nearly alike—it is practice that makes them so widely different." Even his epigrams have a kind of ironical down-to-earthness about them, as though he were disparaging exaltation as well as low morals.

"Don't think yourself so big that other people look small."

"When you see a good man try to equal him; when you see a bad man examine your inmost self."

"Without a sense of proportion, courtesy becomes oppressive, prudence degenerates into timidity, valor into violence, candor into rudeness."

If you want to get the very feeling of the ethics of Confucius, a good way is to remember that as a small boy he had an avid interest in all kinds of rites and ceremonies. He would get a few playmates together and put on a funeral in such elaborate detail that it brought tears to his mother's eyes. He loved music in the same way and learned to sing and play on the lute and zither. In midlife, he traveled to the capital from the small province of Lu in which he lived, in order to study "the rules of music and propriety," and become expert in all the forms of ceremonial behavior. This aesthetic preoccupation colored his ethical teachings. He did not make the profound distinction we do between manners and morals. And maybe he was right. Maybe there is a connection between the rudeness that used to be excused as individuality in our excessively "progressive" schools and the low state of teen-age morality today.

As they grew up, that band of children playing ceremony under his leadership turned into a kind of school. Confucius had to earn his living, and he managed it, as later on the Sophists would do in Greece, by taking in pupils. There was no fixed fee, and none at all if a pupil was both indigent and gifted. But teaching was the business as well as the life-mission of Confucius.

He was a political as well as a moral and intellectual teacher. Like Plato two hundred years later, he drew up the blueprints for an ideal society, though his ideal was very different from the hierarchical system described in Plato's *Republic.* It was essentially the ideal later expressed by the utopian socialists, and it originated, as did Thomas Moore's *Utopia*—if not the whole socialist movement—in the nostalgic wish that society might be like a family. "Men would not regard as their parents only their parents, nor treat as their children only their own children."

The idea was especially utopian in China, because family ties were so close and binding there.

But Confucius agreed with Plato that the only way to move toward an ideal society was to get wise and good men into positions of power. And like Plato he made a great effort to get into such a position himself. Indeed he was possessed throughout life by an ambition to be appointed prime minister by one of the feudal princes surrounding him. One or two of his pupils did receive such appointments, but up to his sixtieth year nothing came his way that measured up, in even the faintest degree, to his world-reforming ambition.

At that time, according to a legend which good manners impels us to believe, he did occupy a minor post in the government of the Duke of his native province of Lu, and he fulfilled his duties so well that a neighboring duke became envious of the resulting almost supernatural prosperity of

Lu. He decided that this too able minister must be got rid of, and devised a rather extravagant scheme to accomplish it. Knowing that the Duke of Lu had two inveterate weaknesses, one for equine and one for feminine beauty, he sent him a neighborly gift of eighty shapely and adorable dancing girls and no less than thirty-four teams of sleek horses. The Duke found both his time and his energy so used up in the enjoyment of these sumptuous gifts, that he couldn't bother to keep appointments with his famous minister. After three or four unapologized-for snubs, the minister hitched up his ox-cart, gathered a little band of his disciples, and departed the province.

He traveled slowly according to the legend, (though how he could travel otherwise in an ox-cart is a question) hoping that the Duke would recall him. But the hope was vain, and Confucius spent the next thirteen years wandering from province to province, seeking another noble lord who would let him put in practice his science of politics. The legends say that he applied for employment to seventy-two potentates, but there are two-and-a-half millenniumsful of exaggeration in all those legends. It is an accepted fact, however, that from the age of sixty to about seventy-three Confucius spent his days traveling through China with a small band of disciples "seeking office." He was received in most states with hospitality, and often with a subsidy, because of his fame, the charm of his company, and his wise counsel. But he was too democratic; he proclaimed (perhaps for the first time in history) that the welfare—

and not only the welfare, but the *happiness*—of the people is the true end of government. "The people are the most important element . . . the sovereign least important." This did not help him find a sovereign who would employ him as prime minister. He was also hindered in this ambition by a certain mannerly outspokenness. At least it is reported that to one noble lord who asked him for instruction on the art of government, he replied with a bow: "The first thing you have to do is learn to govern yourself."

After thirteen years of wandering he returned to his little home-province of Lu, a tired old man, not broken in spirit, but convinced that his life had been a failure. After three more years spent in teaching and editing the ancient odes and histories, he died in that conviction.

Within three hundred years, the record of his sayings, jotted down in mourning by his disciples, and the elucidation of them by famous commentators and apostles, became the substance of all scholarly learning in China. In the 2nd Century B.C., in allegiance to his teaching, an emperor of the Han dynasty established a system of choosing all state officials by competitive examination—a system which survived until the turn of the 19th Century. It was cited as a model for our Civil Service Act of 1883. But by a sad irony, instead of the "all-embracing knowledge" that Confucius had urged upon his pupils, the sole topic of these examinations was the life and sayings of Confucius himself and the scholastic traditions to which they had given rise. Assuredly, this outcome would have dismayed him more than it made him proud, for his bent of mind was scientific rather than academical. Indeed his gospel rested on foundations so similar to modern science that it is hard to believe he was a contemporary of Buddha and Zoroaster. In his emphasis upon flexibility of judgment, upon replacing dogma with the investigation of facts, above all upon suspended judgment, he was thousands of years ahead of his age. He first formulated what might well be described as the Golden Rule of Science: "When you do not know a thing, to acknowledge that you do not know it is knowledge." He thus swept aside the temptations of superstitious and wishful thinking. In describing the essential virtues, the meticulous emphasis he placed upon sincerity—sincerity not only in dealings with others but also in solitary meditation—goes farther in the same direction. There must be no lingering remnant, no last inward glimmer, of self-deception if you are going to travel in the way of truth.

And the way of truth is not "the strait and narrow path" that so alarmed us in our youth. "The way of truth is like a great road. It is not hard to find. The trouble is only that men will not look for it."

I do not mean that he counseled laxity or self-indulgence. He was, on the contrary, a teacher of the morally disciplinary kind. He lashed his pupils with scorn if they were sluggish or lackadaisical about their homework. And the list of qualities toward which they must struggle makes our seven cardinal virtues look rather like a course for undergraduates. The pupils of Confucius must learn to be "quick in apprehension, clear in discernment, of far-reaching intelligence and all-embracing knowledge, fitted to exercise rule; magnanimous, generous, benign and mild, fitted to exercise forbearance; impulsive, energetic, firm and enduring, fitted to maintain a firm grasp; self-adjusted, grave, never swerving from the moderate and the correct, fitted to command reverence; accomplished, distinctive, concentrative and searching, fitted to exercise discrimination; vast, deep and active as a fountain. . . ." To these ideals he added at other times: "gravity," "earnestness," "faithfulness," "kindness," and—sometimes most difficult of all—"a reverent attention to business."

It was not a "snap course" by any means, but it was not alien to man's natural instincts. "The path is not far from man," he cried, "not far from the common indications of consciousness." By which he meant, I venture to believe, not in conflict with our instinctive nature—for one of his most startlingly indicative opinions was that there is not a profound difference between man and the animals.

Being a teacher, he naturally placed a strong emphasis on the virtue of growth. "The most serious of faults," he said, "is to have faults and not try to mend them." There is an upward drive, he believed, in us all—a wish to outdo, if not others, at least ourselves as of yesterday and today. But he seems to have started, as modern science compels us to do, with biological foundations in deciding in what direction, and to what extent, men might sensibly aspire to grow. Many of his precepts take the form of a description of the character and conduct, and even the manners and aspect, of what he called "the superior man"—and the phrase is sometimes translated, perhaps not entirely in a wrong key, as "the gentleman."

"The superior man has dignified ease without pride. . . . Looked at from a distance he appears stern; when approached he is mild; when heard to speak, his language is firm and decided." "The superior man can find himself in no position in which he is not himself. In a high situation he does not treat his inferiors with contempt, in a low situation he does not court the favor of his superiors. He does not murmur against Heaven, nor grumble against man."

In this manner Confucius formulated his conception of the ideals toward which our instinct of emulation ought to carry us. His superior man seems a bit sedate and stately to us. We in America have a more breezy ideal of what a man should be. But that is one of the differences in national culture that make the earth interesting to live on. His basic idea that the ills of the world might be cured, without opposing nature or crying to the gods for help, by getting everybody into a condition of upward growth—this idea has application everywhere.

When one of his disciples reported that he had been asked to explain who Confucius was, the master did not say: "Tell him I am a prophet." "Tell him I am the Messiah." "I am the Son of God." He said: "Why didn't you tell him that I am a man who pursues the truth untiringly, and teaches people unceasingly, who forgets to eat when he is enthusiastic about something, and who forgets all his worries when happy or elated, and is unaware that old age is coming on."

I think the Marxists, with their Religion of Immoralism, will find it harder to displace this simple and supreme teacher in his influence upon Chinese thinking than to displace some of the prophets and viceregents of God who oppose them in other countries.

III

MOSES

THE MOSAIC DICTATORSHIP

We have to dismiss as a myth the pleasant idea that baby Moses was set afloat in an ark, discovered in the bulrushes by Pharaoh's daughter, and brought up as a prince. On that adventure—to speak very disrespectfully—Moses may be said to have missed the boat. For a similar story was told of Sargon of Agade, who founded Babylon seventeen centuries earlier, and of several other great men. Indeed, it seems to have been almost a fashion among national heroes to be launched into life in this picturesque way. If time lasts long enough, a baby Washington may turn out to have been set afloat in a small rowboat on the Delaware River.

Grown-up Moses, however, is now permitted by the scholars to exist in history, and even to enjoy high status among the Egyptians. A recent book, based largely on archeological discoveries, makes credible the whole story of the forced labor of the Israelites under the Pharaohs, and their march into freedom under the leadership of this great man.* Their track through the desert and their conquest of Canaan, "the Promised Land," is followed up, and many places and incidents mentioned in the Bible are identified with sites and physical conditions still existing. The motive of the book is to prove that the Bible is historic, rather than to find out how much of it is historic, but still it sets our mind free to discuss the story of Moses without placing a question mark after every assertion.

The story is a bloody one and it begins with a crime of murder. Moses saw an Egyptian overseer "strike a Hebrew," and he killed the Egyptian. As a fugitive from justice, he fled from Egypt to a land called Midian, east of the Red Sea, and there married and settled down. He stayed long enough to produce two sons. But he was haunted by thoughts of the plight of the Israelites, who, though well fed, were worked to death on the building of palaces and cities for a Pharaoh with a mania for architectural construction. In the end he decided to return to Egypt and try to persuade Pharaoh to set free the Israelites and let them go back to Canaan, which they regarded as their homeland. Pharaoh proved obdurate and, according to the legend, it took a series of ten plagues sent against Egypt by Jahve to induce him to let the Israelites go, and even then he sent an armed force after them and tried to bring them back. (So says the legend. What it more cer-

* *The Bible As History* by Werner Keller, translated by William Neil (1964).

tainly took was a brilliant task of revolutionary organization and political strategy on the part of their leader.) Although it spoils a good story, we will skip the miracle of the Red Sea, and simply say that the Israelites managed somehow to escape into the desert. They spent many years wandering there before they were ready to invade Canaan with sufficient military force to take possession of it, or the better part of it. The Bible says they spent forty years, but "forty" was a number glibly spoken among the Hebrews, and the Moses story adds up better if we make it twenty. At any rate it took a long time to mould that loose band of refugees into a nation, and supply them with an army and weapons, and the military training required to perform a great deed of territorial conquest. Although he dies on the eve of the conquest—and the story from the other side of the struggle has never been told—it is impossible to accept the general drift of it without acknowledging that Moses was a leader of extraordinary force and genius.

Sigmund Freud, in his surprising book *Moses and Monotheism*, makes it plausible that Moses was not a Jew but an Egyptian, as his name would indicate, and was a very fervent believer in the monotheistic revolution initiated by the Pharaoh Ikhnaton in the 14th Century B.C. Freud's hypothesis is that in the anarchy following the death of Ikhnaton and the rabid recoil against his religion, Moses, seeking as it were a following, took up with the enslaved Israelites, and led them out of captivity to continue the worship of the One God. It is an ingenious speculation, but

Freud's story, as it continues, contains so many imagined details that the chance of its coinciding with the facts of history seems to me, as a mere matter of mathematics, rather small.* At any rate, I have no wish to wade into the stagnant swamp of argumentation about such questions. Moses has been described as the inventor of the alphabet, the inventor of preventive medicine, the inventor of monotheism, as a martyr slain by the Israelites, as a medicine man, as a myth, and as the man who established "an indissoluble bond between religion and morality." Although such a bond existed in Ikhnaton's religion, it does seem true that, for the Judeo-Christian world at least, Moses made it indissoluble. That much, I judge, may be called historic.

To me it appears that the establishment of this bond, this notion of an invisible God—and, incidentally, his priests—laying down laws for the regulation of all human behavior, produced a state of mind that, by comparison with other examples of primitive social life, seems almost manic. Much just and even fervently humane and idealistic law-giving is set down to the credit of Moses. But it is mixed with a tense and terrifying passion to control through God's "injunctions, rules, regulations and orders" every curve and intimate ripple of the life of man—espe-

* Martin Buber, the author of another modern book about Moses, dismissed Freud's *Moses and Monotheism* with a scornful footnote: "That a scholar of so much importance in his own field as Sigmund Freud could permit himself to issue so unscientific a work, based on groundless hypotheses, is regrettable." *Moses, the Revelation and the Covenant,* page 7.

cially his sexual life—that takes all the spontaneous joy out of the adventure of being. The notion of a single and invisible God of the universe who had picked out these forlorn refugees from a whole worldful as his chosen people, and was watching over them with jealous and vain and vengeful eyes, seems to have produced in the people themselves a kind of hysteria. They were exalted and frightened. And this enabled Moses, who had a monopoly of communication with this Lone Deity, to establish a dictatorship over them that for absolute control and bloody-handed cruelty has few rivals in history.

Let us examine the record of that political event before astonishing ourselves with the items of just and humane legislation that were so incongruously combined with it.

That Moses could kill, we learned at the beginning of the story, but the extent and ferocity of his killings when he conceived that they were authorized by the word of God spoken to him in private are so terrible that the mind falls shut when the eyes read them. His devout rage when he first came down the mountain with God's commands graven in stone, and found the Israelites worshipping a golden calf, is much admired and was portrayed by Michelangelo in a famous statue. But the massacre in which that devout rage expressed itself is automatically forgotten: "Moses stood at the entry to the camp and shouted, 'Who is for the Eternal? come over to me!' All the Levites gathered round him, and he gave them this order from the Eternal, the God of Israel, 'Sword on thigh, every man of you, and sweep the camp from side to side, killing all your kinsfolk, your friends, and your fellow-countrymen!' The Levites did as Moses ordered, and about three thousand men fell that day." (Exodus 32, 26-28, Moffat's translation.*)

Martin Buber, in his book *Moses, the Revelation and the Covenant,* described this bloody event in the following words:

"Reaching the camp, he summons to him all those who have remained true to Jahve; and these, who belong chiefly to his own tribe of Levi, go forth with the sword at his behest 'from gate to gate' and *reduce all resistance.*" (The italics are mine.) We have been protected in this way, I suppose, by untold myriads of pious Jews and Christians from apprehending the exact size of that pile of corpses.

"Remember the sabbath day to keep it holy," we recite, imagining this to be a serenely pious aspiration which we will try, more or less after our own fashion, to live up to. Actually it was but one item in the ten-point summary of a meticulous series of regulations that were enforced with merciless violence. The teeth of this particular ordinance are to be found in Exodus 31, 13-17: "So keep the sabbath; it is a sacred day for you and anyone who desecrates it shall be put to death. For whoever does any business on the sabbath, the man shall be outlawed. Business may be

* In his famous translation of the Bible into modern English, which I am using throughout these pages, James Moffat substituted for God's name, Jahve or Jehovah, two words, "the Eternal"—a mistake, I think, since it is not a translation.

done for six days, but . . . anyone who does any business on the sabbath, he shall be put to death."

If this decree, which is repeated in Exodus 35, 2-3, leaves any doubt as to whether the penalty was to be death or banishment, the doubt is resolved in Numbers 15, 32-36: "When the Israelites were in the desert, a man was caught gathering wood for fuel on the sabbath day. Those who caught him gathering fuel brought him before Moses and Aaron and all the community, who put him under arrest, as there was no clear law about how he was to be punished. But the Eternal said to Moses: 'The man must certainly be put to death; the community must all stone him to death outside the camp.' So the community all took him outside the camp and stoned him until he died."

"Honor thy father and thy mother," is another gentle-seeming admonition. But here is the manner of its enforcement: "If a man has a stubborn and rebellious son, who will not obey his father or his mother, who will not listen to them even when they chastise him," they shall lay hands on him, bring him before the authorities, and denounce him as "a stubborn and rebellious fellow" . . . "whereupon all his fellow-citizens shall stone him to death. So shall you eradicate evil from you, and all Israel shall hear and fear." (Deuteronomy 21, 18-21.)

That all Israel should hear and fear seems to have been the underlying principle and purpose of all this frightful legislation. Mass terror would be our modern name for it. And the central purpose, we must assume, was to hold the power inviolate in the hands of the dictator, who posed as —and quite probably believed himself to be—the authorized representative of a single and invisible deity. He was accustomed to meet this deity and receive his commands in a "trysting tent" outside the camp of the Israelites, and a cloud was supposed to come and stand before the door of the tent during their interview. Thus no one but Moses himself could hear or see what happened inside. In reading the text, one easily forgets whether Moses is delivering his own edicts or repeating the decrees confided to him in this tent by a supernatural authority. Only two things are sure —the privacy of the communication of God's laws and the ruthlessness with which they were enforced.

In judging Moses, we must remember that he had no promise of a future life—no blessedness in heaven versus torment in hell—to threaten his subjects with. No such idea was current in his day or in the days when his history was written down and revised. The promise of prosperity in this present world as against a flood of inflicted miseries, both for his subjects and future generations, was the only "ideological" argument Moses had. In that respect his religion was no better than Marxism as an instrument of dictatorship. This gave rise (in Deuteronomy 28, 15-68) to one of the most devastating descriptions of earthly affliction to be found in literature, but it did not dispense with the necessity of a large-scale massacre of unbelievers. The very existence of the dictatorship depended on abject obedience to the first Commandment: "Thou shalt have no other gods before me." We may expect, therefore, and we do find, a ferocity in the enforcement of this item that passes every limit of reason or compassion.

We learn in Exodus 22, 20, that: "Whoever sacrifices to any god except the Eternal shall be solemnly destroyed." In Exodus 23, 13, we receive the orders: "Never mention the name of any other god, never let it pass your lips." In Deuteronomy 17, 2 to 5: "If there happens to be any man or woman among you, in any of the townships granted you by the Eternal your God, who does evil in the sight of the Eternal your God, by . . . going and worshipping other gods, bowing down to them or to the sun, the moon, or any of the stars above . . . you must take the evildoer, man or woman, outside the town and stone him to death." And no personal qualms or considerations must withhold you from carrying out this decree. "If your half-brother or your full brother, your son or your daughter, the wife of your bosom or the friend who is your other self, whispers to you the enticing word, 'Let us go and worship other gods' . . . you shall be the first to take a hand in killing him, and then all the people shall follow, stoning him to death for having tried to allure you from the Eternal, your God." (Deuteronomy 13, 6-10).

And if this crime of disloyalty is committed in any of the towns of your own Promised Land, you must destroy not only those who committed it, but the whole town.

To taste the full fury of this dictatorship, and how it surpassed some of the racial and national crimes that have horrified us in our time, we must examine the meticulous instructions that Jahve-Moses issued for the behavior of his armies in their war of aggression against Canaan. In Deuteronomy, Chapter 20, we learn that when they came to attack a town, they were to offer terms of peace, and if the town submitted and opened its gates to them, all the people in the town should be subject to them and do forced labor for them. These were the terms of peace! But if it would not make "peace" on these terms, they should beseige it and when the Lord delivered it into their hands they should "kill every male inhabitant without quarter," and "seize for yourselves the women and children and animals and all the plunder in the town."

This for the towns lying beyond the strict borders of the Promised Land. But in the towns lying within those borders, "which the Eternal your God is giving you for your own, you must not leave a human soul alive; you must put them all to death, Hittites, Amorites, Canaanites, Perizzites, Hivites, and Jebusites. . . ."

It baffles the imagination—even if all this is pseudo-historical big talk—to find items of wise counsel, and even of a very high and civilized morality, mixed with these celebrations of genocide. The juxtaposition seems at times almost consciously ironical. For instance, right after the above counsel of total destruction for their near neighbors, there follows a prudent suggestion that they should take an entirely different attitude toward their neighbors' trees! The text, in Moffat's translation, reads:

"When you are besieging a town for long, attacking it for the purpose of capture, you must never destroy its trees by taking an axe to them. You may eat their fruit but you must not cut them down. Is a wild tree a human being, that you should lay siege to it?" (Deuteronomy 20, 19.)

Indeed it sometimes seems as though in the case of human beings, killing, to Moses, is a quite every-day matter requiring only a certain regulation of the details.

"If any man has committed a sin deserving death, and if he is put to death by being impaled upon a stake, his corpse must not remain all night upon the stake; you must be sure to bury him the same day. . . ." (Deuteronomy 21, 22-23.)

"Fathers shall not be put to death for their children, nor children for their fathers, everyone shall be put to death for his own sin." (Deuteronomy 24, 16.)

In the incident at Shittim, this casual attitude toward human killings becomes especially strange; a single murder, if it is dramatic enough, seeming to equal in redemptive power the massacre of thousands. At Shittim, let me remind you, the Israelites began to "wanton" with the women of Moab, "partaking of their feasts and paying homage to their gods." Moses, on learning of this, "seized all the leaders of the people and executed them in broad daylight." But this "deathstroke," as Moffat calls it, was brought to an end by a private act of murder which seemed horrible enough to meet the demands even of their jealous God. The text reads as follows:

"Now one of the Israelites introduced into his family a Midianite woman and when Phinehas, a grandson of Aaron, saw this, he seized a spear and following the Israelite into the tent stabbed the pair of them, the Israelite and the woman right through the belly. This stopped the death-stroke in Israel, the death-stroke by which twenty-four thousand had died." (Numbers 25, 6-9.)

God had it in mind, the narrator explains, to kill all his chosen people, but Phinehas "by resenting the sin among you even as I resent it," averted God's wrath. Instead of killing them all, he rewarded Phinehas with a "perpetual priesthood," and let the rest, except only twenty-four thousand, go free.

This strange kind of lighthearted reasoning about murder and massacre, a thing not easily associated with any kind of goodness, is to me the outstanding feature of this story of the first "indissoluble union" of religion with morality. Indeed, it is when the deity is most nearly forgotten, and morality speaks, as it were, for itself, that Moses seems to be climbing toward the heights of humane culture occupied by the other great teachers I have been writing about. Here is a kind of goodness that needs no threats or promises from Jahve to back it up:

"You must not keep weights of different size in your bag, and you must not keep measures of different sizes in your house; you must keep a full, just weight, a full, just measure." (Deuteronomy 25, 13-15.)

"When you enter your neighbor's vineyard, you may eat

your fill of the grapes, but you must not put any in your bag. When you pass your neighbor's standing corn, you may pull some ears with your hand, but you must never put a sickle into your neighbor's standing corn." (Deuteronomy 23, 24-25.)

"In reaping your harvest, if you forget a sheaf in the fields, you must not go back to fetch it; it shall be for the alien, the orphan or the widow. . . . (Deuteronomy 24, 19.)

"You must not withhold your help from any ox or sheep of a fellow-countryman which you see going astray; you must be sure to take it back to your fellow-countryman." (Deuteronomy 22, 1).

"You must not hand back to his master any slave who has escaped to you from his master . . . you must not be hard on him." (Deuteronomy 23, 15-16.)

"See that justice is done between a man and his fellow or any resident alien; you must never show partiality to any person in a case, you must listen equally to low and high. . . ." (Deuteronomy 1, 16-18.)

"You must never tamper with a poor man's rights in court. Avoid false charges, never have innocent and guiltless people put to death, nor acquit bad men. You must never accept a bribe, for a bribe blinds even men whose eyes are open. . . ." (Exodus 23, 6-8.).

"You must never repeat a baseless rumor, never side with a bad man to give malicious evidence. You must not follow a majority to do wrong, nor must you bear witness in court so as to side with an unjust majority; neither must you be partial to a poor man's plea." (Exodus 23, 1-3).

"If you have a poor man, one of your fellow-countrymen, in any township of the land which the Eternal your God gives you, you must not harden your heart nor shut your hand against your poor brother; you must open your hand to him, lending him enough to meet his needs." (Deuteronomy 15, 7-9.)

This Mosaic kind of goodness accords so ill with the wholesale ferocities attributed to the dictator that Freud's idea of two men named Moses, one "meek" as the scripture declares, the other arrogantly ruthless, as it depicts him, becomes a refuge against an unbelievable contradiction.* The meeker Moses extends his gentle sympathy even toward animals:

"You must never muzzle an ox when it is treading out the grain." (Deuteronomy 25, 4.)

Saint Paul maintained that it was not gratifying the ox, but paying salaries to Christian ministers, that the Mosaic God was talking about in this famous line. (First Corinthians 9, 9.) But there are other lines which reveal a like tenderness toward animals:

"If you see the ass of a man who hates you lying helpless under its load, you must not leave it all to him, you must help him release the animal." (Exodus 23, 5.)

* I must remark that I find the word "meek" only in the King James version. Moffat has two very different words: "devout" and "pious."

Hate the man, if you must, but don't make the poor donkey suffer! A whole story is contained in that little verse, and it has an affirmative moral. It differs from the Ten Commandments in telling you what to do, not just what not to do.

In an ideal world, most laws, I suppose, would tend to assume a negative form. But the room left open by the laws of Moses for the pleasurable living of life was so filled up with positive injunctions of a merely interfering nature, page after page of specific directions for every affirmative step one might wish to take, that the poor Children of Israel seem to be confined in a ritual playpen.

> They could not boil a breakfast and go to it
> Without some word of God for how to do it.

The one thing that might have been fun for the Israelites in those days, it seems to me, was building the ark for their invisible God to dwell in—an ark so richly jewelled and adorned as to outshine in "conspicuous consumption" not only Aaron's golden calf, but all the idols of all the heathen gods in the whole region. That ark must have given joyful occupation to hundreds of skilled artists and craftsmen and seamstresses. Apart from that, one finds few suggestions in the dreary pages of the Pentateuch of any reason for staying alive except only to arrive at the Promised Land. And that, we must in honesty remind ourselves, meant a bloody war of aggression against five nations and a ruthless butchering of their inhabitants, men, women, children and animals, to the last breathing creature.

In my poem *Lot's Wife,* which is a rather irate protest against the dour and superstitious teachings which I had been brought up to respect, I inserted a sonnet which contained in its fourteen lines ten commandments, each corresponding to one of those in the Biblical decalogue, but having for its guiding theme a healthy affirmation and at least a look toward the joys of life. My sonnet was too artfully constructed, but I think it belongs here where I am sketching my estimate of the kind of goodness advocated by Moses.

"Life's first commandment is that we should live it,
And life is jealous of all meaner gods;
Being implacable, it makes no odds,
Weekday or Sabbath, or what name you give it,
Life will take horrid vengeance if denied;
Honor the givers of it, but more still
Honor the sacred gift; and do not kill—
Your sole right against life is suicide.
Love is life's glow of warmth, and is a giving;
Try, when you love, try hard, not to possess;
Steal only if you steal from death your living;
Admire your neighbor more, and covet less;
And to your neighbor, in both pride and ruth,
And to yourself, for life's sake, speak the truth."

I felt from an early age a lack in the Ten Commandments of any allusion to what seemed to me the prime virtue of truthfulness. In this respect I have learned that Moses was far behind his predecessor in the One-God religion, the Pharaoh Ikhnaton, who regularly appended to the official form of his royal name in all his great state documents, the words: "Living on Truth." Indeed, according to James H. Breasted, Moses was behind the Egyptian moralists of over a thousand years earlier. Breasted quotes, in his momentous book *The Dawn of Conscience,* a "tractate" from the feudal period four thousand years ago, in which the following words are ascribed to an "Eloquent Peasant" addressing the Grand Steward:

"Speak the truth. Do the truth. For it is great. It is mighty. It is enduring. The reward thereof shall find thee, and it shall follow thee unto revered old age." *

In being reminded of the wholesale murders and massacres attributed to Moses, I have, I fear, been weakened in my effort to praise the magnanimity and meticulous sense of justice which actuated him when he was not wallowing in God's rage against heretics. An example of the height to which he could rise above the blind instincts of the herd is his repeated warning to the Israelites, even

* "In such an utterance as this," Breasted remarks in a footnote, "it is important to remember that 'truth' (maat) is always the same word which the Egyptian employs for 'right, righteousness, justice.' "

while he was welding them into a fighting nation, against being arrogant or unjust to foreigners who might dwell among them.

"You must not maltreat an alien, for you were aliens yourselves in the land of Egypt. You know how a foreigner feels." (Exodus 23, 9.)

Another habit of Moses' mind, which even in moments of massacre he could not forget, was the need to determine without error the guilt of a criminal before the dreadful punishment was inflicted. Even when he is dealing death to a whole town for a crime that has been committed within it, this habit of justice makes him demand an investigation that will make absolutely sure that such a crime has been committed.

"If you hear that in any of the towns which the Eternal your God has given you to stay in, some low creatures have broken loose and allured their fellow-citizens with the cry, 'Let us go and worship other gods!' . . . then you must examine and investigate the matter, making a thorough inquiry; and if the thing be true, if it is certain that such an abominable crime has been committed in your midst . . ." then the blow must fall. (Deuteronomy 13, 1-16.)

It would be a relief here to see how this Mosaic mixture of good and evil was transformed by the later prophets of Israel who, though still obedient to the same God—and not, by the way, possessed of power—managed to convert that God into a just judge and even a loving father. But that conception reached its height in the kind of goodness advocated by Jesus, and, for the purpose of this little book, it therefore belongs in a later chapter. Suffice it to say that the Mosaic contrast, or inward conflict, between humane wisdoms and God-authorized bursts of atrocity, did not die with Moses. It recurs more than once in the Holy Scriptures. In Mohammed it amounted to the living of two separate lives. Even in the story of Jesus, the gospel of loving-kindness is interrupted with the threat of a heaven-sent massacre upon any town that would not receive it. That this two-sidedness continued on down through the history of Christianity in Europe is well known.

It is not certain just when the story of Moses was first formally written down—probably not completely until the 9th Century B.C. But it was later subjected to at least two major editings and revisions, and finally to a "priestly codification" in the 5th Century. The purpose of all these textual operations was to improve the lessons it taught, to preserve the laws and make the story of Moses and his God more edifying. Thus the documents as they stand are a thoughtful part of the contribution that this mixture of godhead with morality made to human wisdom at about the time when Buddha was teaching the doctrine of selflessness and the Middle Way, when Confucius was declaring that the happiness of the people is the true end of government, and when Solon, in an effort toward democratic justice, was assembling the entire citizenry of Athens to constitute a law court. The conclusion that morality makes a better start when it is arrived at without the help of a divine overseer seems a natural one to draw.

IV
SOCRATES

SOCRATES: THE HERALD OF LOGIC

He was a funny-looking man with a high bald dome, a small face rather crowded in under it, a blunt nose, wide nostrils, and a beard too imposing for such a perky face. His ugliness was a standing joke among his admirers and he helped them enjoy the joke, for he loved to laugh. He was a poor man, and at a quick glance something of a loafer, though on further acquaintance he turned out to have a keen mind that had mastered the best scientific knowledge of his time. His wife, Xanthippe, is reputed to have had a violent temper and a tongue like a horsewhip, though that has been learnedly disputed. For some reason, at any rate, he loved above all things to leave home.

He would get up before dawn, eat a hasty breakfast of bread dipped in wine, slip on a tunic and throw a coarse mantle over it, nothing elaborate, nothing to button up—no shoes or sandals even in winter—and be off in search of a shop, or a temple, or a friend's house, or the public bath, or perhaps just a familiar street corner, where he could get into an argument. The whole town he lived in was in a constant turmoil of argumentation. It still is, in fact, and that's the trouble with Greek politics. For the town was Athens, and the man we are talking about is Socrates.

He was not only funny-looking, but funny in his ways and notions, and he had a good-natured magnetic stubbornness in sticking to them. For instance, he believed that he carried around with him, almost like a dove sitting on his shoulder, a little private god, who would stop him with a whisper in his ear whenever he started to do anything foolish or wrong. Another notion he had was that the oracle at Delphi had elected him to educate the people of Athens, or rather, since they were bent on arguing all the time, teach them to argue logically. One of his friends had asked the oracle who was the wisest man in Athens. To the astonishment of the whole city, the priestess had mentioned this funny-looking loafer, Socrates. His answer when he heard about it gives a key to his character that has never been forgotten.

"The oracle," he said, "picked me for the wisest Athenian because I am the only one who knows that he doesn't know much of anything."

This attitude of sly and slightly mischievous humbleness gave him a big advantage in an argument. It made him something of a pest, really. For he would go right up to the most prominent citizen, a great orator, or anybody, and ask him if he really knew what he was talking about. Some distinguished statesman, for instance, might wind up a patriotic speech with a peroration about courage, about the glory of dying for one's country. Socrates would step up to the rostrum and say:

"Pardon my intrusion, but just what do you mean by courage?"

"Courage is sticking to your post in danger!" would be the impatient answer.

"But suppose good strategy demands that you retire?" Socrates would ask.

"Oh well, then, that's different. You wouldn't stay there in that case, of course."

"Then courage isn't either sticking to your post or retiring, is it? What would you say courage is?"

The orator would knit his brow and answer:

"You've got me—I'm afraid I don't exactly know."

"I don't either," Socrates would say, "but I wonder if it is anything different from just using your brains. That is, doing the reasonable thing regardless of danger."

"That sounds more like it," someone in the crowd would say, and Socrates would turn in the direction of the new voice.

"Shall we agree then—tentatively of course, for it's a profound question—that courage is steadfast good judgment? Courage is presence of mind. And the opposite thing, in this case, would be presence of emotion in such force that the mind is blotted out?"

Socrates knew from personal experience about courage,

and the listeners knew he knew it, for his cool and sturdy behavior as a soldier in battle was, like his physical endurance and his ability to drink all comers under the table, a matter of city-wide notoriety. He was no mollycoddle! And he had moral courage too. He had defied the public hysteria which followed the naval defeat at Arginusae, when ten generals were condemned to death for failure to rescue the soldiers drowning in the sea. Guilty or not, it was unjust, he had insisted, and moreover it was unconstitutional, to try or condemn men in such an amalgam.

The above conversation was, of course, imaginary. The Greeks had no such phrase as "presence of mind"; the genius of the English language invented that. But it illustrates the essential thing that made this enchantingly frog-faced and persuasive man, Socrates, a turning point in the history of our western, or Graeco-Christian, culture: he diverted the attention of philosophers from problems about the external world to problems of human conduct, but he taught that good conduct is conduct guided by true knowledge.

Temperance, he might say, is a course steered between abstinence and indulgence by a pilot called the mind. Keeping a proper balance between pride and humility, the most difficult of balancing acts, quite obviously requires presence of mind. And so do all the virtues. The good act is the knowing one; it is the act which takes into consideration all the relevant facts, and thinks the situation through objectively and with total clarity. Socrates was extreme and stubborn enough in this opinion to assert that any man who knows the right thing to do, and knows all about it, will as a mere matter of course, choose to do it.

Besides insisting in this extreme way on the moral importance of informed and clear thinking, Socrates took the first step toward teaching men how to think clearly. He introduced, according to Aristotle, the method of inductive reasoning and general definitions. He was, at least, the first to say: "Before we start talking, let's decide what we are talking about."

No doubt this had been said before in private conversations, but Socrates made a gospel of it. He believed, I think, that a millennium would follow if men learned to define their terms and draw valid inferences from them. He was an evangelist and this was his faith. He went about the streets of Athens preaching logic, just as four hundred years later Jesus would go about the villages of Palestine preaching love. And like Jesus, without ever writing down a word, he exercised an influence over the minds of men that a library of books could not equal. His best disciple, Plato, built upon his ideas a whole philosophy of life according to which excellence both in the individual and in the state consists of control by reason. And his grand-disciple Aristotle—Plato's disciple, that is—built on the same foundation the science of logic, a discipline designed to make men expert in this essential moral art of using their brains.

Besides this gospel, which put so high an emphasis on the mind, Socrates believed in another entity which he called the *psyche.* This Greek word had originally meant little more than the breath of life, but Socrates made it mean all that the Christians, when they came along, would mean by the "soul." On this subject his zeal for verifiable definitions seems to have broken down—or given way, at least, before an emotional idea. The soul, he thought—as Plato reports him—was "that within us in virtue of which we are pronounced wise or foolish, good or bad." And he declared this vaguely defined entity to be immortal. That supernatural belief, and his eloquent insistence on it when facing his own death, has seemed to many admirers the supreme thing—at least the unforgettable thing—about Socrates. The new thing, however, and, in the history of human culture, the momentous thing, was his insistence not on the immortality of the soul, but on the everyday logical use of the mind—the association of virtue with valid thinking.

Perhaps Socrates' ardent faith in good logic would not have so deeply impressed the world had he not died a martyr to it. It seems strange to put a man to death for "introducing general definitions." And yet when you think what that new and ingenious technique, when pursued to its conclusions, can do to time-honored customs and traditionally accepted beliefs and emotional notions, it is not surprising. Although to his young and progressive friends Socrates seemed the mildest of men, he must have been regarded as a pestiferous fanatic by thousands of old fogies and even by many thoughtful conservatives. That little private god or "daemon" he carried round with him, which, even to our thought, ill consorts with his gospel of knowledge, must have aroused some extra indignation in those who still honored the gods of their fathers. A conflict not only between faiths but between generations seems to have been involved in his case. For there were two formal charges against him: he did not believe in the gods recognized by the city; and with his teachings he "corrupted the young."

He was tried by a jury of 500 citizens, and condemned to death by a majority of only sixty. Probably very few of them expected him to die. He had the legal privilege, for one thing, of proposing a milder penalty and calling for a vote on that. If he had done this humbly, and with a little respectful eloquence, more than sixty would doubtless have changed their votes. But he insisted on being rational about it. Having maintained that he was a public benefactor, and being also a poor man, he drew the logical conclusion that, instead of death, his penalty should be board and lodging at the public expense! That must have made a lot of the jurors mad. And they probably stayed mad when, after saying that, he relented—not wishing them to confuse reason with fanaticism—and said that, since "Plato here" and some other well-to-do friends had offered to be surety for it, he would propose a fine of 30 minas (in the neighborhood of $120).

The vote went against him again and by a larger majority. But still it was generally assumed that he would escape from prison before the sentence was carried out. The way was carefully left open for him. But again he was stubbornly rational. One of the things I believe in, he said to the disciples who came to him in prison urging escape, is the reign of law. A good citizen, as I've often told you, is one who obeys the laws of his city. The laws of Athens have condemned me to death, and the logical inference is that as a good citizen I should die.

This must have seemed a little cantankerous to his anxious friends. "Isn't that carrying inference from general definitions a little too far?" they protested. And again, although firm, he was not fanatical.

"Where would I go anyway, and what would be the use?" he said in effect. "I'm seventy years old. I can't change my ways and I don't intend to. In other cities the same thing would happen. The young would come in crowds to hear me. The old would put me out just as they have in Athens. Can you imagine me, seventy years old, wandering around the earth being thrown out of one city after another?"

They had no answer, and so they gathered round and prepared their hearts to see their beloved teacher drink the cup of poison. Socrates sent for it himself a little before the sun set over the western mountains. When the attendant brought it in, he said to him in a calm and practical tone: "Now you know all about this business and you must tell me what to do." "You drink the hemlock and then you get up and walk around," the attendant said, "until your legs feel heavy. Then you lie down and your legs will gradually feel numb. The numbness will travel upward and when it reaches the heart, then you will be gone." The attendant spoke warm words of praise to Socrates. And Socrates spoke affectionately of him. Then he did as he had been told, very deliberately and coolly, only pausing to rebuke his friends for sobbing and crying out as though he were not doing the wise and right things. After he lay down, a cloth was laid over his face while the numbness ascended toward his heart. His last thought was of a small personal obligation he had forgotten. He removed the cloth for a moment and said:

"Crito, I owe a cock to Aesclepius—be sure to see that it is paid."

Then he closed his eyes and replaced the cloth, and when Crito asked him if he had any other final directions, he made no answer.

"Such was the end," said Plato, who described this death-scene in unforgettable language, "of our friend, who was of all the men whom we have known, the best and wisest and the most just."

V

PLATO

THE CHAMPION OF INTELLIGENCE: PLATO

When you mention Plato, people are apt to put on a pious expression as though you were going to talk about a saint. But Plato was no saint. He was, on the contrary, if the saintly will forgive my saying so, an all-around man. A prize-winning athlete, a brave soldier, a memorable lover, a poet sensuous enough to be described by Victorian professors as "erotic," a whimsical humorist, a connoisseur of race horses, a convivial feaster, an adorer of slapstick comedy, a man who loved to take adventurous cruises on ships. He lived to be eighty-one and "died at a wedding feast," a fact which history has lovingly preserved because it means that he was full of the zest of life and conversation to the last heartbeat.

All this is important if you want to appraise his teachings as they apply in our time. His times were very much like ours. He flourished in Athens the first half of the 4th Century B.C., when people were tired of wars, disillusioned with revolutions, skeptical of the old forms of faith. They needed some standards of conduct. They were groping for a hold on the real values of life. Plato undertook to find that hold for them. With all his humor, he was as earnest about this as the Hebrew prophets, although he could not back up his findings with an appeal to divine authority. The Greek gods had been a beautiful and charming, but rather selfish and hell-raising crew, who never dreamed of laying down any Ten Commandments. Most of them were too busy with their own pranks and hang-overs to take a disciplinary attitude toward mankind. And while Plato had outgrown the belief in them, and had even begun to talk of God as one imageless being, he did not regard this supernatural being as an authority on human behavior. He had to find both standards of conduct and the reason for adhering to them in this natural human world.

He would never have succeeded in this if he had not become acquainted with Socrates. I have described Socrates as the herald of logic—the prophet and agitator and bringer of the glad tidings of what sound reasoning can do. Plato was twenty when he ran into this epoch-making evangel, and was getting quite a reputation as a poet of the school of Sappho. In one of his love lyrics he made the delicate remark that in a kiss his soul came to his lips and tried to cross over. (That is what the professors call erotic.) He had, besides, two tragedies ready for the stage when he met Socrates. But that pestiferous and lovable crusader for clear reason swept him right off his feet. After a few conversations about the gigantic importance of thinking things out, and the wonders that might ensue if men would only use words with a clear sense of their meaning, Plato went home—they say—and destroyed all his poetry. That was hardly a reasonable thing to do. But maybe it was wise, for the melody of his prose, according to the English poet Shelley, who read him in the original, is "as intense as it is possible to conceive."

Plato adhered to Socrates as student and friend for eight years—that is, until Socrates died. He wasn't a pupil exactly, for Socrates had no pupils. He would no more think of taking pay for teaching sound reason than Jesus would for teaching love. It was a salvation gospel in both cases. But Plato was one of the young men who turned up most regularly at those seminar-like meetings with Socrates at a gymnasium, or the portico of a temple, or the house of a common friend, to have an argument about the meaning of some important idea before drifting back to a saddler's shop to hear the latest news. It meant a great deal to be a friend of Socrates, for next to clear and honest thinking Socrates valued friendship above everything else in the world. It meant so much to Plato that he carried Socrates with him in fancy throughout most of his literary life, writing his own thoughts in the form of conversations in which this moral and intellectual genius played the leading part.

Socrates had tackled the problem of what "virtue" means. He had asked the question why anybody cast loose from the bonds of established tradition ought to be good. And he had decided that goodness is nothing but informed and carefully reasoned conduct. Any man presented with a choice, if he knew all there was to know about it, would choose the right act. It is not necessary to believe this in order to appreciate its importance. For the first time it gave the highest authority upon the most important of all questions to the individual human mind. It was a revolution unparalled in history.

And Plato carried it forward. Not only is the good act the reasonable one, he said, but the good man is the man in whom reason rules. There was no science of psychology in his day, and Plato—never at a loss when invention was called for—made one up. It was a pretty good one, too, and held its own for a couple of thousand years. Our conscious life, he said, is divided into three distinguishable parts: a sensuous part containing the appetites and passions; a restive or mettlesome part which may be called will or "spirit"; and the thinking part, which he called Reason.

Since Reason is what distinguishes men from dogs and baboons, it is obviously the highest of the three parts. It is the one whose natural function it is to rule. The function of spirit is to enforce the dictates of reason. The appetites and passions should obey. Where each part performs its natural function, you have virtue, which is a name for "health, beauty and good condition of the soul." Where this natural order of things breaks down, you have vice, which is "disease, ugliness and weakness."

In this simple way, Plato reasserted, in a time of cynical disillusionment, the authority of the good life. He said in effect that the good life is life itself, sanely and abundantly lived by a creature made as man is made. Truthfulness, modesty, justice, generosity, gentleness, temperance, liberality, courage and honor require no supernatural sanction, and no ulterior reward either in this world or another. They require no sanctimonious emotions—no words like "righteous" or "sinful" or "wicked" or "iniquitous." They need no more defense and argumentation than health does.

"Need we hire a herald, or shall I proclaim the result [of our discussion] that the best and justest man is also the happiest?"

" 'Make the proclamation,' he said.

"And shall I proclaim further: 'whether observed or unobserved by gods or men?' "

"Yes, you had better add that."

Plato's psychology is out-of-date, to be sure, but when you reflect that it was invented when Ezra was promulgating the laws of Moses, you will not be surprised at that. Where Plato said "reason," we say "intelligence," for we realize that knowledge is not acquired merely by abstract reasoning—you have to examine the facts. But Plato's basic idea that integration under the guidance of the mind is the essence of moral character has never become old-fashioned and never will.

Although so friendly to happiness, Plato's rule of Reason could make stern demands. His own creative life required high moral courage, for the whole population and government of Athens were stormily opposed throughout his life to his opinions. In the face of this steady storm, he pleaded for Chabrias, a general on trial for his life, when no one else in town would touch the case. On his way up to the Acropolis with the general, he was met by an intelligence officer.

"Do you mean to say you are appearing for this man? Don't you know that the hemlock of Socrates awaits you?"

"I faced dangers when fighting for my country," Plato answered, "and I will face them in fulfilling my duty to a friend."

In old age Plato became a little irascibly dogmatic in laying down the precepts of Reason, but even then it was the affirmation of life, not its denial, that made him so.

"No man is good for anything asleep, any more than if he were dead," he exclaimed. "*Therefore, those who really care about living and thinking* will stay awake as long as they can, only reserving so much time for sleep as health requires—which is little, once the proper habit is formed."

Energy is expressed there, and Plato's energy is one of the abiding wonders of the world. Though master of all the established knowledge of his time, he poured out a river of original ideas on every subject under the sun. There is hardly a theme or speculation in the subsequent history of philosophy that was not touched upon with penetration in Plato's dialogues. He founded political science with his bold outline of an ideal state, *The Republic.* He talked of mathematical physics and predicted the wonders to be achieved by men like Newton and Einstein. He explained dreams, describing almost in the language of Freud how, when reason's control is relaxed in sleep, suppressed desires peep out, and "the wild beast in our nature starts up and walks about naked."

He talks about the division of labor and the causes of it like a professor of modern economics. He is the inventor—or suggester—of the distinction between higher and secondary education, the necessity of specialization in science, endowment for research, eugenics, non-punitive penology:

"No one punishes a wrong-doer because he has done wrong. Only the unreasonable fury of a beast acts that way. He who punishes with reason looks to the future, and is concerned that those who are punished, and those who see them punished, may be deterred from doing wrong again."

He spoke for the first time (so far as the records go) of the psychology of laughter, acoustics, civil service, the limitation of incomes. (No family, he said, should have more than four times as much as any other.) He invented day nurseries, the kindergarten method—"progressive education"!

"Bodily exercise when compulsory does no harm, but knowledge acquired under compulsion has no hold on the mind. Therefore do not use compulsion, but let early education be a sort of amusement." He also warned us not to carry this notion to the point of abandoning discipline:

"Of all the wild animals the human child is the most intractable, for the fountain of reason in him, being still unregulated, makes him tricky, sly-witted, and insolent in the extreme. Therefore he must be reined in, so to speak, with many bridles."

Plato was known to the ancients as "the first to study the significance of grammar." His pages contain the first example of character study as we have it in modern novels. He described the rise of a tyrant with penetrating skill, giving us a hint that will be useful to us when it begins to happen here: "The tyrant when he first appears will be a protector of the people." He ridiculed "old families," including his own, showing by mathematical calculation that what any individual derives from a remote ancestor, apart from his name, is infinitesimal. He dismissed with a mature smile the notion Karl Marx dreamed up two thousand years later, that moral ideas are a mere expression of class interest. And he is, of course, the original feminist, the spiritual father of the WACS and WAVES:

"Men and women have the same nature in respect to the defense of the state, save in so far as one is weaker and the other stronger."

Now in addition to all this penetrating hard sense—and

somewhat to the obscuring of it in history—Plato had a mystical yearning in him. He wanted to escape from the world of change—from the very existence of those ever-shifting problems to which he provided so early his wise answers. He wanted a religion. And not finding any to suit him in his age and nation, he invented one. Naturally, it grew out of that excitement about the logical relations among ideas which he had caught from Socrates. These ideas that we find so absorbing, he declared, are the true reality; the particular things we see and touch are mere shadows. He even went so far as to say that the idea of beauty is more fun to be with—I paraphrase him slightly—than a beautiful person. Most people find it impossible to believe that a man in his right mind could hold that opinion. And for this reason, posterity has taken "platonic love" to mean not what Plato meant at all, but a purely spiritual intimacy between concrete men and women. Plato himself, we must add, was capable of deprecating the extremes to which his belief in the superior reality of ideas could lead him. "Even the friends of ideas," he remarked in a smiling mood, "are subject to a kind of madness." *

However dominant Plato's gift of mystical belief may have been, it was offset by a rarer gift for leaving things in doubt. It is possible—if you want to—to regard an Ever-

* In *Phaedo,* the dialogue describing the death of Socrates, Plato attributes to him this religion of the superior reality of ideas. But for some humble reason Plato enjoyed putting his own thoughts into the mouth of Socrates, and we are free to form our own opinion as to whether he did so in this case.

lasting Clash of Opinions as the topic and real conclusion of all his dialogues. Many of them raise a philosophic problem, illumine it from various sides, and leave it for posterity to solve. In that, as in his whimsical humor, Plato is alone among philosophers. Many misunderstandings of Plato arise from a failure to chime with his humor, or appreciate his gift of resting his mind in doubt. An age-old example of these misunderstandings is the flat statement, a thousand times repeated, that Plato "banished poets from his ideal republic." The fact is that he toyed smilingly, and in a mood of whimsical self-contradiction, with the question whether our enjoyment of tragic experiences represented in books and the theatre as happening to others, helps or hinders in the building of our own character. He did not settle the question, but left it open.

"There is in us," he said, "a natural feeling which is just hungering after sorrow and weeping, and this feeling which is kept under control in our own calamities, is the same that is satisfied and delighted by the poets. . . . The reflection is not often made that the feeling of pity which has been nursed, and has acquired strength at the sight of the misfortunes of others, will come out in our own misfortunes and can not easily be controlled."

On this ground he very firmly announces that hymns to the gods and praises of famous men are the only poetry which ought to be admitted into an ideal state. But having said this so sternly, he graciously takes it back:

"Let this, then, be the explanation we give of our reasons for expelling poetry, that we have only followed the course of the argument, and let us make an apology to her, that she may not charge us with any harshness or want of politeness. . . .

"I dare say, Glaucon, that you are as much charmed by her as I am, especially when you see her in the garb of Homer?

" 'Yes indeed, I am greatly charmed.'

"Shall I propose, then, that she be allowed to return from exile on this condition—that she is to make a defense of herself in lyrical or some other measure?

" 'Certainly.'

"And I think we may grant a further privilege to those of her defenders who are lovers of poetry and yet not poets. . . . Let them show that she is not only pleasant but also useful to states and to human life, and we will gladly listen, for if this can be proven we shall surely be the gainers. . . ."

That was the challenge with which Plato concluded his whimsical discourse about poetry. Aristotle took up the challenge, and answered it with his famous dictum that the function of tragic poetry is to effect "a purgation of pity and terror." But it could surely be answered in simpler ways—none simpler, perhaps, than that suggested by Plato himself, that poetry be invited to come in and sing us a song.

We ought to remember this smile of Plato's about "following the course of the argument"—a smile that awakens the memory of Socrates—when we approach another of his famously outrageous speculations: that concerning the proper way to organize and run a state. His rapture over logic led him to think that once he had defined goodness in a man, the same definition would apply to the state. As the good man is strictly disciplined by intelligence, the good state must be as strictly disciplined by an intelligent minority. This fitted in with his family traditions, which were far from democratic, and it caused Plato to become the patron saint of conservatives, as well as the spiritual ancestor of radicals.

The austerity with which he put each class of citizens in its place and gave his picked gang of good men the authority and armed force to keep them there, was reactionary. But the measures by which he proposed to make sure the gang would be good—and stay good—were radical beyond measure.

These virtuous and philosophical gunmen, whom he called "Guards," were to have no private property and no private affections. Their wives and children, as well as property, were to be pooled. Their sexual intercourse was to be performed at stated intervals determined by public need, and conducted on eugenic principles as is done in breeding animals. Irregular unions could not be prevented, but the children of such unions were to be destroyed. All the children of a given mating season should call all the parents of that season Mother and Father, and all the other children Brother and Sister. And since they would be removed to state schools as soon as they were weaned, no one would know which is which, or whose is whose. The women, "since they will be clothed with virtue as a garment," would strip and go into the gymnasium with the men. They would also don armor and go to war with them. The children, too, would go to war just to get used to danger and learn by looking on, but they would be mounted on "the swiftest and gentlest horses," so they could get away quickly if their mothers and fathers were killed or vanquished. Meantime, the whole aristocracy, the ruling class, would keep their bodies in supreme trim by rigid diet and exercises, and their minds at the peak of penetration by constant instruction in logic, mathematics, and metaphysics.

Plato did not advocate this communist regime, as many imagine, for the whole state. It was a mode of life for the superior caste designed to make them really superior—in mind and character, as well as power. His perception that this could be done only by selective breeding is startling in its modernity, so startling that to us it reads like a satirical reduction to absurdity of the claim of any mortal class to rule. Our comment would be: "If it takes all that to produce a real aristocracy, let's get along with democracy, unwieldy as it is." But we are not living in the dawn of logic. We lack the smile of faith with which Plato followed where the argument led. Or are we blind, perhaps, to the smile of ironical humor with which he followed the argument so far?

It led him, before he got through, on one of the most

famous wild-goose chases in history. He was sixty years old when, upon the invitation of Dionysius, Jr., the newly seated tyrant of Syracuse, he set out from Athens in a three-banked ship to teach that youthful bounder how to establish an ideal republic. He was met at the dock by the royal chariot and escorted in splendor—some say that Dionysius himself helped drag the chariot—to a suite in the palace. Receptions followed, and banquets—popular celebrations, too, for the masses rightly sensed that Plato, though an aristocrat, would have a mind to their interests.

Plato entered upon his work with rosy hope, but also, alas with prosy thoroughness. The training of the Philosopher-King must begin, he decreed, with geometry. Geometry would teach him that art of close reasoning from exact definitions without which there is no use approaching the more intricate problems of politics. And so it did begin—not only Dionysius but his whole court plunging into this new diversion, until the palace was dusty from demonstrations made by drawing diagrams in sand thrown on the marble floor. Dionysius was so enthusiastic about the reforms to come that when, at some public ceremony, the herald shouted long life to his dictatorship, he cut him off with the remark:

"Stop damning us!"

In short, Dionysius liked Plato, and he liked the excitement. But there was one hitch: he didn't like geometry. The anti-Platonists dug up another philosopher who could prove that tyranny is the best form of government and do it without mathematics. With his help, Dionysius became reconciled to a long life for his dictatorship. He defended it, finally, with a purge of Plato's friends. Holding Plato as a virtual prisoner in the palace, he courted him with lavish gifts and entertainment, trying to get him to back the purge with his authority. But Plato stood fast for justice, due-process-of-law—and geometry. In the end he had to be sneaked out of the palace at night and shipped home by a roundabout route to Athens.*

Plato's life was not empty when he got home after the collapse of this effort to reshape the world. He had already launched another enterprise—seemingly more modest, but in the long run more likely to reshape it. He had founded a school. It was the most famous school in the ancient world, and for that matter in all history. Its sessions were held in a "gymnasium"—or "place for nakedness"—about a mile northwest of Athens. The city had three of these gymnasiums—immense constructions, half park and half pavilion. They contained an indoor ball court and wrestling chamber, an oiling or "rub-down" room, a steam room, hot and cold baths, and dressing rooms (the Greeks called them *un*dressing rooms). Also an outdoor field for track events with benches under a portico for the athletes and a grandstand for the public. And besides that an ad-

* He enjoyed an epistolary revenge some years later when a message came from Dionysius expressing a hope that Plato was not saying too many terrible things about him to his fellow philosophers. Plato reassured him: "There is not so little to discuss that we have to say things about you," or words to that effect.

jacent grove with paths for educational conversation and arcades with recessed seats for those who preferred to take their education sitting down.

In English, a gymnasium is a hall or building devoted to physical play and exercise; in German the same word means a school. In Greek it meant these two things in close combination. And that is where the Greeks excelled us. They were the first people in history—if not the last—who adequately appreciated the importance of the joy to be found in play. They loved athletic sports—not, perhaps, more devotedly than we do, but more devoutly. Their public games were religious festivals—rites performed in honor of their gods. We suspended the Olympic games on account of the first world war, but the Greek cities, when at war, would declare a truce in order to hold the Olympic games. And although Plato could smile at the gods they honored, he must have shared the general feeling that athletic prowess is a sacred, and not just a secularly admirable thing. He would have joined, with a deeper mixture of feelings than ours, in the hero-worship of a modern Olympic champion or an all-American athlete.

The gymnasium he selected for his school was called "Academia," from the Grove of Academus where it had been erected. Its sessions were probably not much more formal than those conversations with Socrates which had been the beginning of Plato's own higher education. There was no tuition fee, no required course of study, and probably a lot of fun—for Plato could even teach geometry with a smile. Moreover he was at ease among the athletes, for, according to a tradition that no one has confuted, he was twice a Pan-Athenaic champion in his youth. Platon (which means *broad*) was a nickname tacked on him by fellow athletes in admiration of his fine shoulders; his sedate professional name was Aristocles. On the whole, it is doubtful if anything less "academic" ever existed in the name of education than Plato's school in the Grove of Academus. But the school survived all the other uses of that particular "place of nakedness." It survived just under a thousand years, and gave to all the languages of Europe the words *academy* and *academic.*

We must remember that there was no Sunday in Plato's time, and no Sunday school. There was no institutional tendency to separate ethics from athletics. Plato would not have known what to make of the long, frail, languid, ineffectual saints that populate most of our church windows. The contrast between what we admire and love to have around us, and what we call "good" would have been incomprehensible to him. The notion of life in this world as a "preparation" for life in another where standards of excellence are different would have astonished him; no one in his circle had a father, or a grandfather, or a great-grandfather who had ever heard of that humiliating notion. They all instinctively assumed that the values of a good deed are cashable here and now. If they pay in a future life too, so much the better, but they will pay in the same coin. When Plato says: "What shall it profit a man if he receives gold and silver on condition that he enslave the best part of him to the worst?" he means it as a downright matter of good bookkeeping based on psychological science.

There is, to be sure, a very vital lack in Plato's teaching that integration under the control of the mind is the whole essence of good character. His code, as he left it, was designed for a supposedly superior class in a society served by slaves, a class which looked upon foreigners as "barbarians." We find something ingrowing and provincial about a goodness, however heroic, which is concerned with organizing the inward parts of a single man. Sympathy of one man for another, a sympathy of each man for the whole population, was something Plato never thought of. That came into our western world with Jesus and the Christian Evangelists. It came in a form that flatly opposes Plato. The good man is not ruled by reason, according to the Christian code, but by a passion—that of love for his fellow men.

No need to recall how deeply this new teaching affected the world. Plato, if confronted with it, might also have been deeply affected. I think he might have said, after some years of meditation: "You are right, I failed to realize the high place occupied by sympathy, or what you call love, in the good life, and in the character of the good man. But you are wrong in thinking it can be made the ruling principle in morals. You have only shown that it is intelligent to cultivate sympathy, and even carry it to the point of granting equal rights to slaves and barbarians. But you cannot show that it is anything better than intelligent. You cannot show me that self-sacrifice may not become a vice, that pity does not need like any other passion to be held within rational bounds. It is still reason, it is still intelligence, that rules."

Thus Plato might have demonstrated his high and abiding place in our western philosophy of life.

VI
MOHAMMED

THE TWO LIVES OF MOHAMMED

Unlike Jesus, whom none of his adorers took the trouble to describe, Mohammed left an image in history. He was "of middle height, greyish, with hair neither straight nor curly; with a large head, large eyes, heavy eyelashes, reddish tint in the eyes, thick-bearded, broad-shouldered, with thick hands and feet." He was "in the habit of giving violent expression to the emotions of anger and mirth." But he had also a commandingly infectious smile, and is remembered as a gentle and friendly person, full of good fellowship—"never the first to withdraw his hand from a handshake." The words suggest great personal magnetism, and of that he was undoubtedly possessed, for the manner in which, with a belated start at fifty-odd years of age, he won over all Arabia to his faith and his political dictatorship, is not short of prodigious.

It becomes still more prodigious when you know that up to the age of forty he had made no mark at all except as a good businessman, the proprietor (seemingly) of a store which sold agricultural produce. He was, however, a judicious and reliable man, the kind you would go to for advice.

He was born about 569 A.D.—well born so far as status goes, but orphaned in babyhood and brought up by an uncle, whom he accompanied on camel caravans from their native town of Mecca to Syria and southern Arabia. When he grew to manhood he was employed by a rich widow named Khadijah whose wealth was invested in the camel trade. He proved so good a businessman, as well as so attractive a youth, that she, although fifteen years his elder, proposed a "matrimonial partnership." He proved to be a good husband as well as a good partner. They had four daughters, and as long as Khadijah lived he was faithful to her. At least he took no other wife, although he took a lively nine of them after she died.

Nothing in the story so far suggests the coming to mankind of a prophet sent by God, much less a prophet with outstanding administrative and military genius. We must infer, however, that Mohammed employed a great deal of the leisure supplied him by Khadijah's wealth in pondering the old question of the why and whither of human life. He was pained by the poverty and misery of his people, their tribal wars and blood feuds, their ignorance even of the scattered bits of the Hebrew and Christian religions which he had picked up—either by word of mouth or by the desperately hard work of reading, for he was no man of books.

It has even been asserted that he could not read or write.

In his late thirties, he began to spend whole days and nights alone on a mountain near his native city of Mecca, fasting and seeking some revelation of the true values of life. Most civilized nations had at that time what may be called a spiritual belief: Buddhism, Christianity, Hinduism, Confucianism, Zoroastrianism. But Mohammed's people, the Arabs, mostly nomads or recently settled tribes, were just passing from the worship of "stocks and stones" to the worship of the countless demonlike deities, male and female, supposed to dwell within them. They had a small, square temple in Mecca which they called Kibbah which is said to have housed as many as 360 idols. To these their worshippers made pilgrimages from time to time, and this troubled Mohammed's deeply religious and impetuously active mind. He had learned from the Bible to despise idol-worship, and think of the one invisible God and his angels as a power that would save the Arabs and make them equal to the more civilized nations with whose merchants they traded. He dwelt on this so long and with such fervor there on his mountain top, that he fell at last into a trance and saw clearly before him a messenger from God. Indeed it was the angel Gabriel, the same that announced to the Virgin Mary the coming birth of Jesus, who appeared on the mountain and stood right in front of him. Addressing him in his own language, the angel bade him recite some words couched in the rhymed sing-song employed by professional soothsayers among the Arabs:

"Recite! in the name of the Lord,
Who created man of a clot of blood.
Recite! Thy Lord is most gracious,
Who taught by means of the pen,
Taught man what he knew not."

To us the words seem rather more puzzling than inspiring, but the presence of the angel was so solidly real that Mohammed was thrown into a violent perturbation and repeated his words in high excitement to Khadija. She, in turn, reported the event to a friend well versed in the Hebrew Bible, and he, upon this rather slender evidence, assured Mohammed that he had been called by the One God to become His prophet to the polytheistic tribes of Arabia.

It was a big order for a man past forty, and it took courage of both the knightly and the saintly kind to accept it. But the hallucinations continued; the trances proved easy to reproduce; the angel was always there to dispel moods of doubt. Gradually Mohammed became convinced that the rhythmic sayings of God's messenger were the chapters of a book existing in heaven and "sent down" to him for the information and salvation of his people. He was the divinely elected successor of Abraham and Noah and Moses and Jesus—all the prophets he had heard or read about. And he had the force to declare that where his account differed from theirs, their record had been falsified—his authority was final, his was the last word of God. Together with this force of character, he had mental gifts which, though untrained, were extraordinary, for he could remember and repeat to his friends the rhythmic words that he heard spoken in each trance. These words, hastily written down by his friends, constitute the chapters of the Koran —or "recitation"—the Bible of the Mohammedan religion.

Thomas Carlyle called the Koran "as toilsome reading as I ever undertook: a wearisome confused jumble, crude, incondite; endless iterations, long-windedness, entanglement . . . insupportable stupidity, in short!" This, although he was defending Mohammed's sincerity and making him the protagonist of his essay on "The Hero As Prophet." More recently, Dr. John Alden Williams of McGill University informs us that no translation of the Koran, however faithful to the meaning, has ever been successful. In Arabic, he says, the book is "by turns striking, soaring, vivid, terrible, tender and breathtaking." He gives seven pages of examples from Professor Arberry's translation, which he describes as "the only one in English which has succeeded in suggesting the extraordinary qualities of the original." I find some eloquence in these pages but nothing to warrant any one of the above exciting adjectives. Either Dr. Williams is right—the Arabic is untranslatable; or Carlyle is right—the book is a bore. After laboring along in a standard translation for the better hours of several days, I find myself in more and more firm agreement with Carlyle.

It does not matter very much. The Arab people were on

the rise in mind and body, and they needed a religion that would combine well with national patriotism—later on, indeed, with the assertion of a right to rule the world. Mohammed knew his people, and whether by instinct or by deliberate intention he chose those aspects of the Judeo-Christian religion which would appeal to their childlike passions. He did not try, as Moses had, to bring them to the One God and his commandments without offering them the reward of a future life. He borrowed from The New Testament the idea of a Day of Judgment, a heaven for those obedient to the law, and a hell for those who disobey. Those who obey shall enjoy every sensuous pleasure; those who disobey—or still worse, *disbelieve*—shall broil in fire forever.

In the details, however, Mohammed's God was a little less demanding than the God of the Hebrews. In his version the Biblical doctrine became somewhat less rigidly austere. "God is minded to make his religion light unto you," he said, "for man was created weak." And although, with a single exception, he himself stood fast by the One God doctrine, he did not demand too much of this steadfastness from his disciples. Finding one of them in tears because he had been driven by cruelty and abuse to deny his faith and make prayers to the idols, Mohammed asked: "But how dost thou find thy heart now?" And when the disciple answered: "steadfast in the faith," he said: "Then if they repeat their cruelty, thou mayest repeat thy words."

Although this disposition to soften the moral demands of

religion, to make exceptions, to allow for mistakes and forgettings, to play up the role of *intentions*, is to be found throughout the Mohammedan scripture, the attacks that Mohammed himself made upon the idol-worshippers of Mecca were crisp and unqualified. He was a bold and strident reformer—a madman, as it seemed to them. He endangered his life, and if he had not belonged to the leading family of a powerful tribe, there is little doubt that he and his babble of the One God would have been put out of the way by physical means. He was indeed on a certain occasion so frightened that he publicly belied his own faith, stating that he had learned from Gabriel that two of the goddesses worshipped by the Meccans might conceivably make a successful intercession with the Supreme Being. He was, however, filled with remorse for this loss of fortitude, and soon reported that in another trance God's messenger had explained that the previous words had been dictated by Satan. With that one momentary lapse, Mohammed lived in Mecca a life of inflexible consecration to his one God evangel that places him among the heroes of religious history. In three years of steady and intrepid preaching, he won only forty converts, and after ten years he had but a hundred-odd. His uncle Abu Talib was the head of the family to which Mohammed belonged, and when it was intimated to this man that if he did not muzzle his nephew there were those who would, he appealed to Mohammed to moderate at least his threats of hellfire for unbelievers.

Mohammed replied: "Though they gave me the sun in

my right hand and the moon in my left, to bring me back from my undertaking, I will not pause till the Lord carry my course to victory, or I die for it."

With that he burst into tears, and his uncle was so moved that he promised to stand by him, although not himself a convert to the new religion.

To understand this overpowering conviction, I think it is necessary to remember that Mohammed was not only a religious, but a moral reformer. His devout and vivid belief in the One God, combined with the more egotistical satisfaction of believing himself to be God's only living prophet, was reinforced by an iron faith in his visions. (Only a course in modern psychology could have bent or broken that.) But besides that he was shamed by the primitive and dirty and deprived and bloody-handed lives lived by his people. He wanted to see the Arabs catch up with their more civilized neighbors, and I suspect that the morals he preached drove home the religion almost as much as the other way round. He taught them to wash—both their persons and their garments. He taught them to be just, to be patient, to be kind—"God loves a kind man"—to be humble—"Hell is the resort of those who are too big with pride"—to stop stealing, to have respect for property rights and for the rights of women in marriage. He denounced slander. He denounced usury. He preached temperance and hard work. Both drinking and gambling were sins according to his code. So was extravagance, so also was miserliness. He raged, as did Moses, against one sin that is now little but a memory—the killing of unwanted female babies. Above all, and most insistently, he demanded the giving of alms to the poor. That the poor might in justice not always be with us, is a revolutionary idea that never occurred to him. Charity was, in his teaching, almost the essential virtue, so redeeming in its nature that with enough of it one might purchase redemption for many self-regarding sins. One might even purchase redemption for the sin of a transitory physical love.

All prophets of God, as though surmising that religious fervor is a sublimation of sexual passion, seem to have fulminated with special fury against what they have called—in order to take the last glint of poetry out of it—by some such name as "fornication." And Mohammed, so far as morality in this world goes, was like the other prophets. But he knew the Arabs, and it was for them that he invented his religion. Instead of the light which beams so unquenchingly in every image of the Christian paradise, he promised the pious among these desert-dwellers—he promised them, every time their future life was mentioned—*shade!* And walking in this shade, he promised an abundance of black-eyed maidens "with swelling breasts," and with no memory of the word fornication.

Up to his fiftieth year, what I have written seems to have been the essential story of the life and teachings of Mohammed. At that point, however, events occurred which would change in a profound way the whole drift of his thoughts and his influence. The first of these events, and to my thinking one of the most important, was the death of Khadijah. If a wise book should ever be written about the great women who have stood behind, and often somewhat above, great men, I feel sure that Khadijah would occupy a distinguished chapter. Fifteen years his senior, and with wealth enough to employ him and enter into their passionate friendship as his boss, she must to an unusual degree have replaced the mother he never knew. Her death, it seems certain, left many of his emotions on the loose. And very soon after that, another thing happened that changed his drift as determined by the pressures around him: the death of his influential uncle and protector, Abu Talib. I do not mean that he lost heart in the new solitude; he remained inflexible in his denunciation of the idols, his preaching of morals and the One God. But the torrent of outraged hatred rose more strongly against him. The merchants of Mecca were reaping a big harvest from the pilgrims that came every year to worship those 360 idols in the midst of their city, a factor which has been offered by the priests of economic determination as an explanation of the violence of their hatred of this One-God fanatic with his strict rules of conduct. All we know is that in another two years they made life in Mecca unendurable both for Mohammed and for his little saintly band of followers.

The city of Medina, 247 miles away, having a considerable population of Jews and no such violent objection to monotheism, offered them a hospitable reception, and to save their lives—or at least make them endurable—Mohammed's followers fled from Mecca and trekked across the desert to that city. Before joining them, Mohammed outwitted a plot to assassinate him by hiding three days in a cave to the south of Mecca. July 16, 622, the date of his departure from Mecca to Medina—the Hegira, or Flight, as it is called—was subsequently taken as the beginning of the lunar calendar that is used in all Mohammedan countries. The day was, indeed, momentous in the history both of Mohammed himself and of his religion, for he was received with enthusiasm by an influential body of the citizens of Medina. They were at the moment uneasy in a truce between two clans that fought for control of the city, and were in need of a mediator. Mohammed's trait of good judgment caused him to be chosen as arbiter in this and other disputes that arose among the citizens, and he soon climbed—with the help of his supernatural connections—to a position where he was able to declare himself by law the sole judge and arbiter of all disputes. From there it was not a long way to a brilliantly organized theocratic dictatorship; it was not a long way to absolute power.

A saying of Lord Acton's that power tends to corrupt, and absolute power to corrupt absolutely, has had currency of late, since history has offered us so many new illustrations of it. No illustration is more perfect than the life-story of Mohammed. It is in fact two stories, as James Freeman Clarke made clear in his once-famous book *Ten Great Religions:*

"From the Hegira the Mohammedan era begins; and from that point in his history the prophet's fortunes rise, but his character degenerates. He has borne adversity and opposition with a faith and a patience almost sublime; but prosperity he will not bear so well. Down to that time he had been a prophet, teaching God's truth to those who would receive it, and by the manifestation of that truth commending himself to every man's conscience. Now he was to become a politician, the head of a party, contriving expedients for its success."

He had preached against stealing, but one of his early expedients was highway robbery. Indeed he supported his party through its early troubles with brilliantly organized raids on caravans carrying goods to Mecca; he bought the support of the big shots of Medina with a part of the loot. Another expedient was to raid established cities that would not acknowledge his One God religion, and pile up their wealth in the coffers of his party. Of course he was not without a Divine warrant in this; every step was taken at a bidding he received in a trance from the messenger of Allah. But between his normal self and the self that spoke to him in these trances, the distinction was becoming more and more confused. In the end we find the God of the Universe issuing a judgment as to the best way to settle a quarrel that had arisen among the oversupply of wives in his harem.

Both these selves found it expedient to demand of the disciples one thing above all—submission. The word *Is-*

lam means submission, and it occurs so often in the preachings of Mohammed that it has become in popular usage a name for his religion and for the whole body of believers in it. "Man should be as passive in the hands of God," he taught, "as a corpse in the hand of him who washes it." But it was not primarily God—much less fate or the turns of fortune—to which one must in this corpselike way be "submissive," it was the dictatorial police state with which Mohammed united the tribes of Arabia, and set out to conquer the world. For of all the messages brought down to him by the angel Gabriel, the most momentous, both for his history and the history of the world, was the news that God wanted him to propagate the faith by fighting. It resulted in the discovery—unsettling enough without God's backing—that he was not only a master of political administrations, but also of military strategy, a skilled general, a warlord. When, after a prayer to the One God for victory, he defeated with 300 men an army of 900 sent against him by the Meccans, he awarded himself (by a special revelation from the same God) a fifth part of the booty. And he further awarded himself the death by execution of two personal enemies among the Meccans.

"Who will take care of my little girl?" cried one of them.

"Hell fire!" replied Mohammed, and had him cut down.

In the sequel he became so "big with pride" that after a witty woman poet wrote satirical verses about him, he gave public praise to the disciple who murdered her when asleep with her child in her arms. He gave express command for the murder of an aged Jew who committed the same literary crime.

His high hopes for the educated Jews in Medina turned into fighting hate when they refused to accept his unscholarly version of their scripture and acknowledge him as the sovereign prophet of God. After a victory in battle, when 700 of them surrendered unconditionally, he herded them into the public square and had them executed one by one from dawn until evening. Their wives and children he sold into slavery, saving only one, the most beautiful, whom he added to his harem. These bloody and horrible deeds were recorded by contemporary Mohammedan historians with a mind to glorify their prophet.

We must remember, however, that Mohammed learned these modes of behavior, together with most of what he knew, from the Hebrew scriptures. An example will be found in Ezekiel 9, 5 and 6, where "the splendor of the God of Israel" bids a man with an inkhorn go through the city, put a saving mark on the foreheads of all who are opposed to idolatry, and gives orders to destroy the rest. "I heard him say . . . : 'Follow him through the city and strike, without mercy or pity, kill old men, young men, maidens, children, women—kill them, kill. . . . Pollute the temple, fill the temple-courts with corpses, then out to the city!' So they went off to kill throughout the city."

This was one kind of goodness held out to Mohammed as an example by "The Splendor of the God of Israel" in the only religious book with which he was acquainted. He was also acquainted, however, with the gospel of Jesus, whom he regarded as at least one of the prophets of God. It seems to have been power alone that corrupted him. With power in his hand, his religion became, as Goethe remarked, "a means rather than an end." It became a means to the consolidation of the Arabian tribes into a single all-conquering and all-plundering nation. The words of the Koran which best served that end do possess, even in the English translation, a certain raw eloquence:

"The sword is the key of heaven and of hell: a drop of blood shed in the cause of God, a night spent in arms, is of more avail than two months of fasting or prayer; whosoever fails in battle, his sins are forgiven: at the day of judgment his wounds shall be resplendent as vermillion and odoriferous as musk; and the loss of his limbs shall be supplied by the wings of angels and cherubim."

By such words, as Edward Gibbon wrote, "the intrepid souls of the Arabs were fired with enthusiasm; the picture of the invisible world was strongly painted on their imagination: and the death which they had always despised became an object of hope and desire." *

Mohammed himself was attempting to carry his "holy war" beyond the borders of Arabia when he died at the age of 63. And within a hundred years his successors had conquered in the name of "the One God and Mohammed his Prophet" a good half of the known world—from Per-

* *The Decline and Fall of the Roman Empire,* Chapter 50.

sia to the Atlantic coast, and from southern India to beyond the northern tip of Spain. So completely had the ecstacy of power corrupted and swallowed into itself the naive aspirations of a good man.

To one examining the Koran, and contemplating the deeds of this neurotic and savagely cruel old man, this might seem a disaster—almost an end, or a dreadful suspension, of the progress of civilization. The fact, as we know, was opposite to that. Art and science flourished in the Moslem half of the world—factual and theoretical knowledge, conscientious scholarship, research. The Arabs preserved the intellectual and cultural treasures of civilization throughout the ages when they languished and almost died in Christian Europe. If you ask why this shoddy, unpoetic and unlettered copy of the Biblical religion could have occupied so high a place, I can think of only one answer: supernatural beliefs are not of determining importance in the life of man.

VII
JESUS

JESUS AS A HUMAN TEACHER

Several things make it difficult for me to get acquainted with Jesus, as I have with other teachers of the good life. The Sermon on the Mount, that eloquent summary of his early and more happy teachings—so startling in its beauty and rebellion against vainglory and the pride of power—I was compelled to learn by heart before going to church on a series of unwelcome Sunday mornings. This pretty nearly destroyed for me both its poetry and its penetration. My brother's brain or tongue was more nimble than mine, and in a contest he would come in with a lead of several verses after giving me a handicap of three beatitudes. Even now those vividly arresting words lie beaten down like a racetrack through my mind. It requires a special stimulus to make them stand up and mean something.

On the other hand, my mother, who was not responsible for this Sabbath-day exercise, loved Jesus with an unorthodox yet fervent love; and I loved my mother. I learned from her to think of Jesus as in all respects, though not a divine, yet an ultimate teacher of the wisdom of life. His words, when they came to life on her lips, were not merely advice and inspiration, but almost a creed. This removed them in another way from my spontaneous appreciation. Thus, both by a Sabbath-day discipline and by the week-long fervors of my heart, I was deprived of a simple, friendly-critical, smiling acquaintance with this wonderful man, or tradition of a man.

A thing that helped me to overcome this numbed condition was to read the story and words of Jesus in the modernized and yet not smoothed-down translation of James Moffatt of Oxford. Moffatt did not make the mistake of confusing modernization with reduction to the commonplace, as so often happens. It is a besetting sin of translators, when they find a startling word in the original, to replace it with a humdrum word in the translation—a natural result of their concentration on the task of making an alien thing intelligible. Moffatt, it seems to me, did not make this mistake. He abandoned the antique cathedral beauty of the King James Version without sacrificing the vigor and surprises of the original. The cathedral is still there, and can be entered when ceremonial grandeur is relevant or is wanted. But in my new effort to become acquainted with Jesus, I have found it helpful to read the story in the everday language of my own time.

A more fixed obstacle, of course, is the belief of Jesus himself, tenaciously clung to by his followers, that he was something above judgment—that he was a god, or still more baffling, the son of God. The persistence of this belief among educated men, though seemingly quite accidental in its causes, has echoed far beyond the walls of the church which was founded on it. Even those who reject the myth of his godhead approach the teachings of Jesus with a faith or fury that was born of the myth. Nietzsche denounces his gospel in an ecstasy of italics that discomforts the reader as would the screams in a madhouse. And Tolstoy, though also rejecting the myth, barely escaped the madhouse himself after trying to swallow down the gospel as a complete, unanswerable solution of all life's problems.

There is so much astute hard sense in Nietzsche's *Anti-Christ,* and so much valid aspiration toward a more gentle wisdom in Tolstoy's *My Religion,* that some casting up of the balance would have seemed natural, the two books having been written within the same decade and not many miles apart. But each one is locked in a thought-proof chamber; those who revere the one rarely if ever approach the other. Such insulation from the stream of sober reflection and emerging good judgment was a predictable result, I suppose, of Jesus' own conviction that he was divine and was due to return in clouds of glory very soon—"I tell you the present generation shall not pass away before this happens"—to "despatch his angels with a loud trumpet-call to muster his elect from the four winds, from the verge of earth to the verge of heaven." (Mark 13, 27.) What could not have been predicted is that this spectacular idea, with its roaring noise and glory-imagery, should have captured the sober minds and imaginations of the most advanced sector of the population of the earth, and held them transfixed for twenty generations—although the passing of one generation was sufficient to demonstrate its fancifulness.

Another obstacle to my effort to draw near to Jesus is the inconsistency of his teachings as they have come down to us. A distinguished New York publisher once asked me to write a book on the question whether Christianity had done more harm or good in man's history. The answer would have to begin, I judge, by drawing a distinction between the Mosaic threats sometimes uttered by Jesus and his gentle teachings of nonresistance. The distinction is made instinctively by Christian ministers and Sunday School teachers. They do not mention—especially in our day when bombs from the sky have caused such unspeakable devastations—that Jesus called down such a devastation from the sky on any town that should fail to welcome the teachers of his faith. "I tell you truly, on the day of judgment it will be more bearable for Sodom and Gomorrah than for that town." (Matthew 10, 15.)* We can, of course, join Tolstoy in weeding out all such criminal proposals and denying arbitrarily that Jesus ever uttered them. But there is no scholarly warrant for it. There is no warrant at all, un-

* "The Eternal rained sulphur and fire from heaven on Sodom and Gomorrah, sweeping away these towns and all the Jordan basin, with all the inhabitants of the towns and whatever grew on the ground." (Genesis 19, 24-25).

less we also join Tolstoy in his almost psychotic need for a single, self-torturing doctrine that should wish away all his problems of conduct. When Jesus made a whip of cords and drove the money changers from the temple, an act of riotously violent resistance to evil, Tolstoy's *Gospel in Brief* tells us it was only the cattle and doves that he drove from the temple. But you need no whip to drive cattle; all you have to do is slap them on the flank. To my mind the picture of Jesus becoming enraged at the commercial prostitution of the temple and going in there with a gang of his more able-bodied followers and cleaning the place up is too momentous to pass over. His performance was insurrectionary, and almost as inharmonious with an ethic of nonresistance as his calling down of heaven's hydrogen bombs on every city whose gate-keeper refused to admit his delegates. It is an unconvincing kind of nonresistance that burns people in hell for not believing in it.

There are other troublous contradictions in the teachings of Jesus, and in the sketchy record of his life and behavior. There is hardly another great man except Shakespeare about whose life so little is known—so little, indeed, that several respected scholars have maintained that the whole story is symbolic, that no such being ever lived. It seems highly improbable to me that so complexly unique a record could have been constructed out of whole cloth, or such acute and beautifully spoken precepts invented with no substance to build on. But I do find my search for an authentic Jesus obstructed by the glaring inconsistencies in his quoted words. His lovable bold humanizing, for instance, of the harsh and bigoted laws laid down in the Mosaic code as against his declarations of obedient adherence to that law: "Ye have heard that it hath been said, etc., . . . but I say unto you. . . ." This gentle-revolutionary break with the absurdity and negativism of some of the old ordinances that derived their authority from life-fearing superstition, chimes badly, or chimes not at all, with the protestation: "Never imagine I have come to destroy the law or the prophets; I have not come to destroy but to fulfill. I tell you truly, till heaven and earth pass away, not an iota, not a comma, will pass from the law until it is all in force." (Matthew 5, 17-18.) It was another way of saying: "I am, false reports to the contrary notwithstanding, no heretic, but an orthodox Jew."

The recent decision of the Roman Catholic authorities that the Romans, and not the Jews, were responsible for the death of Jesus, though motivated by present social pressures, accords, apparently, with the most probable reconstruction of the facts. Crucifixion was a Roman mode of execution, and Jesus was hanged on the cross with a Roman sneer above his head: "The King of the Jews." Omitting motivated elaborations, it would seem that he was executed for attempting, or at least proposing, to inaugurate a kingdom of the Jewish God in defiance of the power of the idolatrous Romans. Certain High Priests of Judaism no doubt stood in with the Roman power, and it must have been in revolt against them too, and their commercialization of religious prestige, that he seized the Temple. This must have complicated the story and made such elaborations plausible.

By elaborations I do not mean deliberate falsifyings, but distortions and shifts of emphasis due to the needs of the evangelists who were attempting to found throughout the Roman empire a church based on the worship of a Jewish God and redeemer. I pause to recall that the chief competitors of this God and redeemer were not the exalted pagan deities, Zeus, Hera, Athena and the others, sitting aloft on Olympus, but the lesser gods, the patrons of fertility, who were worshiped by plain people at secret conclaves called "mysteries." The whole content of these secretive celebrations has never been explicitly revealed, but in all known cases, the death and resurrection of a god was symbolically represented. Adonis, Attis, Osiris, Dionysius, Demeter and Persephone—they all died and were reborn in these cermonies, which symbolized the withering of the fields and gardens in the autumn and their rebirth in the spring. They not only symbolized, but were supposed in some mysterious way to cherish and promote that rebirth or resurrection. Surely the thought was not always absent from the minds of those participating in this celebration of resurrection in the abstract, that they too might be reborn. Sir James Frazer, who described all these things in his discerning and beautiful book *The Golden Bough* said something in this connection that has a special interest for us today.

"When we reflect how often the church has skillfully contrived to plant the seeds of the new faith on the stock of the old paganism, we may surmise that the Easter celebration of the dead and risen Christ was grafted upon a similar celebration of the dead and risen Adonis, which, as we have seen reason to believe, was celebrated in Syria at the same season. The type, created by Greek artists, of the sorrowful goddess [Venus] with her dying lover in her arms, resembles and may have been the model of the Pietà of Christian art, the Virgin with the dead body of her divine son in her lap, of which the most celebrated example is the one by Michelangelo in St. Peter's." *

Now the founders of the Christian Church had, or believed they had, the memory of a real death and resurrection to offer in competition with this symbolic performance. Not only the crops should rise again, but the worshippers themselves should be guaranteed a future life if they believed in this personal god who, although not presented to their eyes in a ceremony, did on a certain date actually die and rise from the dead. That was the doctrine upon which St. Paul and his followers founded a new religion—not a Jewish but a world religion, a step, as they thought, from primitive myth to downright reality. It will not matter now, but to them in those days it was important that the Son of God should not be represented as too loyal a Jew. In this they were indignantly opposed by those of the disciples who after the crucifixion had "returned to Jerusalem

* *The Golden Bough,* abridged edition, Vol. I, p. 401.

with great joy, and were continually in the Temple blessing God." (Luke 24, 52-53.) These more quiescent believers were not founding a church, and not inventing a "Christology," but as pious Jews were continuing to fulfill the law while embroidering on the miracles and awaiting the second coming of their Lord. To join their group it was not enough to believe in the divinity of Jesus; you had to accept his Jewishness; you had to obey the law; you had to be circumcised.

The conflict between these two groups or sects was angry and bitter, and while it does not, alas, enable us to choose between them, it does at least explain the two kinds of Jesus presented to us in the gospels. The very extremism of his declaration of adherence to the law makes one feel that this was put into the record by someone in a heat of argument. I permit myself to believe that the "humanizing" Jesus is the more authentic.

A more stubborn contradiction is that between his reliance upon God to explode the sky, ordain the judgment day and establish his kingdom, and his militant announcement that it would require fighting, and that he himself was ready to take arms. He was "advocating violence"—that is evident, and was evident two thousand years ago, especially to the chief priests and pharisees he chastised so relentlessly.

"Blessed are the peacemakers"—yes, but: "Never imagine that I have come to bring peace on earth; I have not come to bring peace but a sword."

Some fifty years ago, when I was editing a radical socialist magazine, much was made among us of the alleged proletarian agitator in Jesus. One of our issues was thrown off the subway newsstands in wrath because, in celebration of Christmas, we had Christ's head on the cover, and the caption: "He stirreth up the people." An editorial of mine in that issue entitled "The Church is Judas" did not mitigate our crime.

It still seems to me that there are two Jesuses in the tradition: one a fighting rebel, the other a pacifist who hopes by advocating humility and the love of the neighbor, to prepare men for a supernatural coming of the kingdom.

"Resist not evil, but overcome evil with good." That wonderful sentence from a man who came "not to bring peace but a sword!"

The conflict may never be resolved, but it has been set somewhat at rest in my mind by a recent book, a scholarly and deeply reasoned book, by Joel Carmichael, entitled *The Death of Jesus.** Carmichael recalls that the Jewish concept of the "Messiah"—a transcription of the Aramaic word for king—was, in the time of Jesus, a political as well as a religious concept, a slogan of colonial revolt as well as a promise of supernatural salvation. And he advances the idea that Jesus first conceived of the coming of the kingdom in purely moral and religious terms, but that after he decided to go up to Jerusalem, influenced by the vast crowds who followed him as an emancipator, he was

* Oxford University Press, 1962.

swept along into their more political view of his mission. Somewhat unexpectedly he seized the Temple and took the leadership of that "insurrection," which is mentioned casually in the biblical account of his trial.

Whether Carmichael's hypothesis is valid or not—and who shall ever decide?—it clarifies a contradiction that must otherwise imply a neurotic conflict in the inmost character of Jesus. There were in truth two Jesuses, just as there were two elements in the concept of the Messiah, but they did not coexist. They were the same multiple-gifted man at different moments in his career—a career which, starting in almost a pastoral mood, rose with such dizzying rapidity to the brief fateful tragedy of the trial and crucifixion.

It is important to admit this contradiction, for history is full of sword-bearing rebels, but no one of them except Jesus gave to our western conception of morals—left so hard-headed by Plato and Aristotle—the ideal of universal sympathy or loving-kindness. That is the great good thing that, notwithstanding the fragmentary and belated memoirs in which his teachings were enshrined, Jesus contributed to our treasure-chest of wisdom. In answering my publisher's question whether Christianity has done more harm or good, that would be the key point, I think, on the good side.

On the other side stands the fact that thanks to his teachings—and to the Jewish culture out of which they arose—he robbed the western world for two thousand years of the frank and unblushing, and, therefore, sane and temperate, sensuality of the Greeks. The rigid puritanism with which Christ's most humane and reasonable talks are hardened has, in my opinion, worked a corruption of two thousand years duration in the hearts of men.

"I tell you, whoever divorces his wife except for unchastity commits adultery; and he who marries a divorced woman commits adultery." (Matthew 19, 9.)

Can we ignore the housefuls of woe and cruelty and spiteful hate that have been added to the sum of human misery by that remark?

Even the disciples protested:

"If that is a man's position with his wife, better not marry at all!" they cried. (Matthew 19, 10.)

He answered: "True, but this truth is not practicable for everyone, it is only for those who have the gift.

"There are eunuchs who have been eunuchs from their birth, there are eunuchs who have been made eunuchs by men, and there are eunuchs who have made themselves eunuchs for the sake of the realm of heaven. Let any one practice it for whom it is practicable." (Matthew 19, 11-12.)

I am quoting from Moffatt's translation, and I pause to say that the *New English Bible* smooths this all down as follows:

"That is something which not everyone can accept, but only those for whom God has appointed it. For while some are incapable of marriage because they were born so, or were made so by men, there are others who have themselves renounced marriage for the sake of the kingdom of Heaven. Let those accept it who can."

There is no allusion to God or his "appointing" in the Greek text of the *New Testament.* Nor do I find there any disguising of the word eunuch, which means in Greek what it means in English. Can this be a deliberate perversion, a bowdlerizing of the scripture, by the translators of the *New English Bible*?*

That ideal of abstention from intercourse with women must have been sustained by floridly passionate friendships among men. The whole Mediterranean world of those days, I judge, was a man's world. The picture of Jesus and his twelve male companions, one of them spoken of as "the beloved disciple," wandering about Palestine together, must ultimately provoke the interest of our all-inquiring psychologists. They can not fail to observe that there is at least a scenic similarity between the story of the Last Supper and Plato's Symposium. Jesus himself seems to have shocked all twelve of his companions by his disposition to address women as equals, and by that immortal sentence: "Let him who is without sin among you cast the first stone." As he had already declared it a sin to look with lust upon a

* The King James Version has it this way:
"All men cannot receive this saying, save they to whom it is given. For there are some eunuchs, which were so born from their mother's womb: and there are some eunuchs, which were made eunuchs of men: and there be eunuchs which have made themselves eunuchs for the kingdom of heaven's sake. He that is able to receive *it,* let him receive *it.*"

woman, we may well understand his certainty that no stone would be cast.

His magnanimity toward women, which raised him not only above the disciplinary laws of the Jews, but above the folkways of his time, stands in sharp contrast to the extremism with which he condemned the least flicker of extramarital desire in a man. It seems here, and at some other times, as though the distinguishing feature of his gospel, the crux of its divergence from the wisdom of the Greeks, was, not to curb or regulate, but to deny absolutely the most indubitably hereditary instincts of man. Love your enemies—take no thought for the morrow—do good to them that misuse you—if a man strikes you on one cheek, offer him the other—if he tries to steal your cloak, hand over your coat-and-vest besides—if your eye bothers you, being prone perhaps to gaze desirously on some young girl's shapely body, pluck it out and cast it from you. All this is so complete a rejection of natural instinct that one can make a formal declaration of belief in it without experiencing any genuine compulsion to live it out. And that, no doubt, is one of the reasons why, for centuries, so many billions have accepted it as an absolute law of life. Its unqualified edges suggest the divine, and it is for that very reason obviously not to be lived up to by the run of men on earth.

There is little of this unlivable extremism in the great moral teachers who preceded Jesus. The laws of blessedness that Buddha laid down were sufficiently extreme to give rise to a cult, and so afflict mankind with another priesthood, but they are not essentially anti-instinctual; they have provided many normal men with the framework of a fruitful and happy life. Indeed Buddha's self-assertion began in a revolt against all life-killing asceticisms. And so of Socrates, Confucius, Plato and the rest. But Jesus, we must remember, is the only one of these uplifting spirits who believed that a day of judgment was in immediate preparation. His moral instructions, though at times they rose into the sphere of universal wisdom, were predicated upon that primitive and passing notion. They were directives as to the proper preparation for his prompt return in glory to save the good and condemn the bad to everlasting torment. It does not seem preposterous after two thousand years to suggest that since he was wrong about this, some of his other pronouncements might be modified a little, and some additions made.

One of the additions the Greeks would make is a word or two in favor of the virtue of courage. Although both Jesus and St. Paul had plenty of it, there is no demand for it in their teachings. I mean courage to face the terms of life as it has to be lived. Imagine asking someone else to shed his blood for you. Is not that a request that goes with a self-pitying and wailing kind of ethics? For me there is too much consolation in the Christian conception, too little of the Emersonian gospel of self-reliance.

"Save me, O my God!"; "Hear me when I call"; "Have mercy upon me, Lord." These and similar outcries are unknown, so far as I have observed, in other religions. Likewise the motherly saying that was so dear to Kierkegarde: "Come unto me, all ye that labor and are heavy laden, and I will give you rest." The consolation offered is not for any particular misfortune, but for the hazard that reality itself presents. It is not so much a weak as a craven state of mind. And it reaches a natural climax in the cry-baby philosophy called Existentialism, with its "anguish" and "forlornness" and woe over the "absurdity" of the "human situation"—at best a drying of tears and a great summons of morale to face the obvious fact that you are born and will die, and must live life for its own sake or not at all.

Notwithstanding this softness in the gospel of Jesus, and his superstitious belief that he was God's son and was coming back in splendor and glory to establish a kingdom, it can not be denied that he brought a new and inestimable jewel into the treasury of wisdom handed down by the Greeks: a thought of the very high value of humbleness about oneself and sympathy for others. The more gaudy his superstition—the more "glory," I mean, in the burst of clouds and lightning amid which the kingdom was to be established—the more arresting is the news that those destined to have high place in his kingdom were the unassuming, the kindly, the forgiving, not the proud ones, not the high and mighty, not the priests or nobles, not even the heroes. Perhaps these ideas were not wholly new, except to the western world. Perhaps they were only oriental, and Christ's service was to give them a poetic expression. He did give them a uniquely poetic expression, however—so poetic that they are woven forever into our concept of a good man.

"Blessed are the meek, for they shall
inherit the earth!"

Was it not a dire misfortune to mankind that such an ideal for a good life on earth should be associated with self-advancing fantasies about getting into heaven? I have preserved through the hazards of my education enough ignorance of history so that nothing prevents my imagining that the gentler teachings of Jesus, with their unique poetry and penetration, might have become known throughout the Mediterranean world without the claim to godhead. Neither Buddha nor Confucius, nor indeed Mohammed—nor even Zoroaster, so far as we know—performed miracles or pretended to be divine. In this respect, they exemplified the humility of spirit that Jesus taught. Socrates, to be sure, had a "demon" whispering in his ear, but this seems to have been regarded as an eccentricity rather than a proof of his importance. The *Golden Sayings* of Democritus were famous among lettered men wherever Greek was read, and Democritus, the "laughing philosopher," was as far from theurgy as a mind could reach. The Stoics filled the Mediterranean world with their austere doctrine of antipatriotism and the Brotherhood of Man, though their god had little more to do with human affairs than to sum them up.

Judea was a tiny nation, to be sure, in most respects a backward one, and Jesus seems to have taught mainly among the unlettered classes. Still it does not seem outlandish to imagine that his golden sayings, like those of Democritus, might have made their way into that wider world without the help of miracles. He himself, according to the gospels, did not enjoy performing miracles; he did not like that kind of publicity. And this helps me a little in my exploit of imagining that he had no need of them. He might have spoken his parables and preached his morally and poetically revolutionary sermon effectively without a supernatural overestimation of himself.

THE CARDINAL VIRTUES: AN UN-SABBATH-DAY SERMON

THE CARDINAL VIRTUES: AN UN-SABBATH-DAY SERMON

With the exception of Confucius, the great teachers of virtue have based their codes upon some supernatural belief. Buddha, to be sure, was not a believer in God, but his notion that good deeds are rewarded and bad punished throughout an endless cycle of reincarnations was remote from matters of fact. Even Confucius, the least mystical of moralists, hinted that there was some counterpart in an impersonal "heaven" for the rules of good conduct which he thought should prevail on earth. And Plato, although his moral teaching was offered as valid for this world, could not forbear to reinforce it with a myth of rewards and punishments in the next. As for us moderns, we quite commonly associate virtue with piety, with otherworldliness, with concern for the immortal soul. And yet I venture to think that throughout history, if a test could be devised, the skeptics would be found to excel in simple goodness the true believers.

Coming of a tribe of Christian ministers, I have always felt the temptation to compose a sermon—I mean, earnestly to advocate good conduct. And I wonder whether it might not be done without any surviving trace of the notion that things are something else than what they are. The text might be from Horace, or Ecclesiastes, or from Robert Herrick: "Gather ye rosebuds while ye may." The theme would be that the most difficult virtues are essential to the rich experience of mortal life. They require no supernatural sanctions; they derive their authority from common sense and the method and results of science.

There are in the traditional view seven cardinal virtues: courage, prudence or mindfulness, temperance, and justice, according to the Greeks; and to these the Christians added faith, hope, and sympathy—or in their language, love. The list would be revised somewhat by a preacher who believed in matters of fact and scientific thinking, but it would not be abandoned.

Not a sparrow falls to the ground but proves that there is no Divine Providence, no Oneness of All Life. Every little bird is distinct and must take care of itself. Under these circumstances courage is absolutely necessary; it needs no heavenly argument. And physical courage is not enough, either. It does not make something of life, but only enables it to proceed. Moral courage, or boldness in asserting one's self, is just as important. Those who think they imitate Christ or the Buddha forget that Christ and the Buddha were not imitators. To imitate them is to abandon their high example.

But courage itself may be a danger. Such courage as theirs may lead to the madhouse, if it is not disciplined by thinking. Presence of mind, as Plato and our English speech perceived, is the larger thing we want when we ask a man to be brave. Presence of mind should stand first when the talk is of morals, for it is only as mindful beings that we are subject to moral instruction at all. It should also come last, for when all the ideal principles have been learned, it remains to decide in each concrete situation which one is to be applied. Once the irreducible variety of the world is acknowledged, and is embraced as an opportunity, we can no longer live by any code. In every crisis we must think out what is good. Even pure impulse and abandon may at times be good, but only the thinking man knows when. Even a lie, in emergencies of small range, may have value, but all the consequences must be measured and known. For honesty flows also from presence of mind, if the mind in question has any scope. The cheat, the liar, the evader is in the long run cut off from the true delights not only of social communion, but of communion with himself—for what self has he left? He is cut off from reality almost as fatally as if he had not been born.

To be mindful of others is a little less obviously necessary than to be mindful of ourselves. It involves more effort, and is more often supported by appeals to supernatural authority. Carried to the point of loving our enemies, it does badly need such authority. But when kept within sane bounds and given its true name of imaginative sympathy, this Christian virtue is nothing more than reasonable. Gregarious by nature, we consist largely of reverberations, and cannot reach our own stature without taking into ourselves the experience of others. Taking thought for others is a great joy; it gives life that genial flow and backflow that make a game as well as an ocean of it. It satisfies also to the extent possible our solemn wish to be one with the world. There is no oneness except such as we create, and we create it by living in imagination the lives of all creatures. The prophets derive a false sentiment of love from the concept of unity or the fatherhood of God, but it is multiplicity and the orphaned condition of man that make real sympathy and kindness both indispensable and rewarding. Such sympathy begets tolerance, a virtue that has been strangely lacking among the devotees of the religion of love. It also begets humbleness, for no man fully alive to the prides of others can be overly proud of himself. More carefully, I should say that it begets, or makes possible, an equilibrium between the extremes of pride and humility, of tolerance and the intolerance that life also at times requires of us.

Thus even in the virtues, even in taking thought for others, we must be temperate if our aim is mortal life and not salvation from it. True temperance is unknown to the saints, for sainthood itself is an intemperance. But its need is obvious to those who live with fact and reason. It flows logically from a wish not only to avoid the death dealt by indulgence, but to possess aboundingly the joys of life. For these joys are diverse, and each requires a separate energy and an unspoiled taste. A man who has reveled to excess in one pleasure lies below ground in the ditch of it, and cannot see, much less explore, the kingdoms of this world and the glory of them.

Justice, I think, flows almost inevitably from the union of Greek with Christian ideals. The Greek word so translated did not mean all that we mean by *justice.* In Homer it meant "the way." It was the way things were done. And when disputes arose, if they were not to be settled by fighting, this way had to be decided by some judicial procedure. Applied to the decision thus arrived at, the word came to mean not merely the customary, but the right way, or "rightness." It still meant "rightness"—or was traveling the road between "rightness" and "justice"—when Plato defined it as "everybody attending to his own business." He so defined its institutional aspect, meaning that every member of a class in his ideal state should perform the function proper to that class. And within the individual, he found the same word to mean "each part of him performing its proper function." This makes very little sense unless the word is translated "rightness." And what Aristotle has to say on the subject makes even less sense. It seems clear that the concept of justice as it stands in our minds did not exist for these philosophers. It did not come into being until Christianity had popularized in the West the ideal of sympathy, of doing to others as you would that they should do to you—or as Confucius more circumspectly put it, "not doing to others what you do not want done to yourself."

Justice, then, might be defined as the verdict of reason when sympathy is generalized. It does not demand that we love our neighbor as ourselves, an abnormal achievement and one that depends very largely, and quite properly, upon our neighbor. It demands that we judge our neighbor as ourselves, that we recognize both in private affairs and public institutions his equal right to build a life. That is high enough and hard enough, but it is a standard toward which we can aspire without becoming abnormal. And it has the same terrestrial authority as reason and sympathy, the Greek and Christian standards from which it was derived.

So far, then, my sermon follows the old sound track. No matter how mortal and matter-of-fact we become, up to this point the tradition of the cardinal virtues stands firm. A courageous, self-reliant, mindful, just, honest and temperate man, combining rational intelligence with kindly sympathy and the modesty and tolerance that go with it, is useful and beautiful on this earth, both to himself and others, and need not look to heaven either for justification or reward.

At this point, however, the tradition goes astray. To a mind dwelling resolutely on this earth, neither faith nor hope in the Christian sense is a virtue. If faith means believing in momentous ideas not supported by sound reason or convincing evidence, it is the first sin to be condemned by science. In faith's service every depraved and unsocial impulse of man has been given a function of honor. Faiths, being otherwise undetermined, make handy disguises for the lust of power and, so employed, have filled all history with cold, brutal and triumphant crime. If every man who ever kneeled to drink of an unverified belief had stood firm in the morale of suspended judgment, that, more than any miracle or revolution, would have led mankind toward paradise. We must raise into faith's place the discipline of doubt, of poised experimental thinking, if we are to live better, or live well, in this finite flux which is the only thing we know. To suspend judgment until facts are known requires courage; it invites thought; it makes room for sympathy; it gives time for justice; it is the supreme test of self-restraint. It has certainly a more natural place among virtues than faith.

And hope, too, is alien in this rigorous company. Hope is too fluid, and spreads too easily into self-deception and sentimental optimism, to be allowed a high place among virtues. Santayana's acceptance of unflinching disillusion is nobler in the mind. It was not hope in general, however, that Paul urged with such pathetic vehemence upon the early Christians. It was the one fixed hope of joy in heaven, a very immediate hope to him, but a hope useful only in abstaining from the joys of this earth. It was a hope of indemnification, and was never otherwise defined by that brilliant yet neurotic apostle. Paul shows none of the friendliness toward present pleasure that makes Jesus so stalwartly sweet and is so intrinsic to his gospel of imaginative sympathy. It is the fate of all great-hearted teachers to be distorted by some unbalanced disciple. But few epigones in history, I suspect, have done mankind the damage Saint Paul did with his strident emphasis on the privative aspects of Christ's teaching.

"Those who belong to Jesus the Christ," he shouted, "have crucified the physical nature with its propensities and cravings." It was to support this continuous act of suicide that Paul made such a frantic fuss over hope as an abstract idea—a hope which "reaches up secure and strong into the sanctuary behind the heavenly curtain where Jesus has gone before us." It is well to remember that Jesus was already gone when this fixation upon hope as a significant virtue came into being. Until we purify our hearts of this sin against life, purging away every inclination to associate virtue with the renunciation of carnal delight, we are not healthy enough, not well-balanced enough, to live wisely in this world.

To replace, then, that heavenly decoy, hope, I am compelled—since committed by the form of my sermon to the number seven—to seek out a virtue more akin to nature and more conducive to health. Voltaire, in attacking the philosophy of optimism, put work in the place of hope, having thoroughly murdered the latter with his slashing pen. "Work, then, without arguing," said Martin. "It is the only way to make life supportable." And Candide agreed with him in a famous epigram: "We must cultivate our garden." Goethe came to a similar conclusion, although with an influence from the Christian gospel. Faust found his moment of happiness in digging canals designed to benefit the community in which he lived.

Work is indeed, like play, one of the most important things in this life. It is the only cure I have ever found for melancholy. And philanthropic work, if one happens to be philanthropic, is, I suppose, an especially fair way out of the clutches of this devil. A great many sanitariums have flourished on these principles, and the reason is not far to seek. To labor toward some end throughout the energetic hours is the normal condition of all animal life. Walt Whitman was wrong when he said, in praising the animals: "Not one is . . . industrious over the whole Earth." Even the lark must collect her ninety or a hundred bugs a day. That is reason enough for regarding work, and the having of a work to do, as an element of good hygiene. A robust man, however, wants to aim at something more stirring than his animal origins. He wants something better to inscribe on his banners than a medicine.

Growth, I think, rather than work, would be the scientific candidate for hope's place among the virtues. To one seeking the best without spurning his foothold in nature, growth seems almost the inevitable crown of the virtues. To grow continually without growing old—that is affirmative, dramatic, difficult. It is something that only man can do. It is the sole way, without being unnatural, to surpass nature. The Greeks have but one word for these two ideas, nature and growth. And the Chinese, I am told, write the word *not* by drawing a straight line over a plant as though everything had to grow in order to affirm itself. But plants and animals grow only to the point of maturity, and then stop short or begin to recede. Man, having a mind, does not have to stop growing. He can understand what nature does, and extend without abandoning her ways. He can cultivate the garden of himself, a wisdom as simple as childhood and as native to the earth.

It is a wisdom much needed today, when so many are surrendering their selfhood to a state or a party, not through poverty or insecurity, but because they no longer know what to do with a self. They have lost confidence in the old supernatural directives and do not know where to turn for guidance in living a life. Had they known from tradition that every man has a duty to grow—had we the custom, for instance, of saying "What are you learning?" instead of "How do you do?"—they would not so lightly surrender to any exterior discipline the happiness to be found in doing this duty.

That is what fact and reason have mainly to say, it seems to me, about morals. A man who knows himself and knows the world, whatever his attitude to the mystery of the universal, needs no God and no Sunday-school teacher to tell him to be good. If he preserves, together with mindfulness, courage, sympathy, temperance, justice and the art of inquiry, the gift nature gave him of growth, he will live well, and with good luck will live happily; and when his time comes to fall to the ground with the sparrow, he will know that he has made a jewel of the accident of his being.

THE REALITY OF CHOICE AND JUDGMENT

A very old difficulty arises for those who put their faith in science rather than religion. It is the assumption of science that every event has a determining cause. If this is true of such an event as what we call a conscious choice, the idea of choice seems to be a delusion. What is chosen was determined, not by our will, but by a whole series of antecedent causes. This makes moral standards seem irrelevant and superfluous. If a judgment about present facts is determined by antecedent causes, then not only moral choices but scientific findings seem to lack validity.

I once discussed this question with no less an authority than Albert Einstein, and I think my record of our conversation will make clear—or at least make more interesting—what I am now trying to say:

I told him with the boldness of my youthful days as "assistant in philosophy" at Columbia that I thought he talked about the universality of causal determinism with too much assurance. The principle cannot be profitably abandoned in performing a scientific experiment, I said, but if generalized it destroys the validity of all scientific judgments.

"If a mind is determined in its judgment by antecedent causes, then it cannot be determined by the reasons upon which its judgment is supposed to be based."

Einstein had evidently never thought of that. He grappled with the idea delightedly, as though it were some kind of game we were playing. After a few random parries and thrusts, he said:

"We view the situation in one aspect when we say that a whole process is caused, and in another when we say that a mind is judging on the basis of the evidence."

"But that is merely a dodge," I said. "If you are going to be philosophic, you can't leave the ultimate truth with two aspects."

He assented to that, but countered it with the difficulties involved in the notion of free will. I admitted that this notion seems of little more ultimate use or validity in describing the situation than that of universal cause. A scepticism about the power of the human mind to solve any ultimate problem honestly confronted is all the philosophy I have, and like other negative positions it is not hard to defend.

The argument was long and meandering, and we did not, of course, reach any conclusion, but it ended in his explaining my position to Infeld* in German with great clarity and force. What he said exactly was:

"He means that if a judgment is merely a fact, then it cannot also be a truth."

"It sounds so good when you put it in German," I said, "that now I am perfectly sure I am right."

To which he replied with a beaming smile, and we changed the subject.

I have, since that conversation, found or invented a way out of this difficulty, which may perhaps be merely a personal tunnel of escape, but which will at least be hard to refute. The most enduring mystery about reality as science apprehends it is how a material process in a brain can become, or give rise to, an immaterial mind. Spinoza, being obsessed by the being of God rather than the behavior of men, imagined a universal "parallelism," and no interaction between mind and matter. Thomas Henry Huxley, more in the spirit of biology, spoke of mind, or consciousness, as an "epiphenomenon," and seemed to regard it as rather accidental. It would be more in the spirit of present day biology to say that, while the question *how* it arose is beyond penetration, the reason *why* a conscious mind arose was its survival value to the organism which should possess it. Its function was, by delaying the instinctive responses and weighing the merits of different modes of behavior, to make a more perfect adjustment to the environment than an unconscious brain can.

* His collaborator in a book called *The Evolution of Physics.*

It would accord well with this view of the origin of consciousness to imagine that another equally momentous thing happened: The delayed responses were set free, within limits, from the causal sequence, so that the organism might, in actual fact, choose that better adjustment. Only on these terms, it seems to me, could this epiphenomenon, this extraordinary device of conscious thinking, be a genuine advantage to the evolving organism which gave rise to it.

I have perhaps only added together two unsolved problems—mind-and-matter, free will-and-determinism—without solving either one of them. But in a very special sense they belong together. They are equally insoluble, and in combination they no longer conflict with our instinctive ways of thinking and talking. So far as conscious thought enters in, we can continue to regard the future, although limited, as not wholly determined by the past. There are genuine choices, judgments, hazards, dramatic fatalities, just as all conversation and literature—also all scientific deliberation—assume there are. Moral standards, like the rules of logic, although they arise in a causal nexus, are of determining importance.

APPENDIX